a little taste of…

japan

a little taste of...

japan

Recipes by Jane Lawson
Photography by Alan Benson (recipes)
and Gorazd Vilhar (location)
Additional text by Charlotte Anderson

MURDOCH BOOKS

contents

a little taste... 6

noodle bar 8

izakaya 30

fish market 62

vegetable market 104

home-style cooking 142

yoshoku 202

kissaten 228

basics 244

glossary 248

index 253

SPECIAL FEATURES

noodles **16**   yakitori bar **38**   sake **46**   sushi bar **72**
seaweed **88**   vegetarian food **110**   pickles **126**   o-bento **134**
rice **152**   festival foods **170**   soy **192**   tea **236**

a little taste...

History, culture, religion, geography and climate have shaped Japanese cuisine into one like no other in the world. The cuisine has developed over many centuries as part of a splendid and complex civilization, initially influenced by continental Asia, but refined in its very own way.

Around the foundation of rice, a wealth of dishes are created utilizing the freshest of ingredients. Vegetables and produce from the sea predominate, while meat appears far less often and only in small quantities. Foods are prepared with a light hand, and their natural flavours and textures are emphasized. Sometimes ingredients remain raw, transformed only by stylish slicing and presentation. The cooking techniques of simmering, steaming, grilling, deep-frying and pickling are all quite simple, yet in Japanese cuisine they are handled with a special touch. Flavours are typically delicate, rarely obvious, and never overpowering; instead they play on complementary tastes and subtle combinations. Many foods are eaten at room temperature, which is believed to further enhance flavour. The taste of soy sauce is commonly present, also a slight sweetness born of the syrupy rice spirit, *mirin*.

Even shapes are said to have a 'taste', for Japanese cuisine considers the eyes as well as the palate to be important. Ingredients are cut into pieces—not only does this make them easy to manage with chopsticks, but the variety of interesting shapes also provides visual appeal. The typical

Western presentation of large portions of several foods all heaped on the same plate, the sauce from one running into the others, seems unappealing, even abhorrent, to the Japanese, who are accustomed to small portions, each in its own serving dish, with its own particular flavour or melange of flavours.

Because the serving dish is chosen to enhance the food within, rather than simply contain it, this varied cuisine calls for a rather large and eclectic assortment of small plates and bowls, in different shapes, colours, patterns and materials. Skilled artisans have been meeting this demand for centuries by producing pottery, porcelain, lacquerware and basketry of astonishing beauty. Even inexpensive, everyday, factory-produced tablewares are frequently handsomely styled as well.

The seasons have a strong influence on the ingredients chosen, dishes prepared and serving utensils used. The garnish chosen to complete the artful arrangement of food on the plate also reflects the time of year, with perhaps cherry blossoms in spring, a dewy sprig of bamboo in the heat of summer, red maple leaves in autumn, or pine needles in winter. It is truly a singular experience to behold the way all of these elements come together on a table beautifully arranged with a *kaiseki* banquet, the pinnacle of Japanese cuisine.

a little taste of...

In Japan, noodles are nearly as popular as rice, and that is really saying something. Every village seems to have at least one noodle bar, towns can have dozens of them, while Tokyo alone has thousands. At their most basic, noodles are sold from *yatai mise*. Once very common, these wheeled carts still set up in the early evening on corners all over the business districts. They sell simple, hot, filling and cheap noodle snacks to fortify hungry salarymen for a night out on the town or to stave off hunger until they eat dinner at home. More established noodle shops can be found in or near almost every train station, in department stores and food arcades, and along any street. Some are basic *tachigui* bars where patrons stand while they eat, others have stools or booths but remain quite utilitarian, while still others are decked out in a rustic style of dark wood, indigo textiles and pottery. The best of these noodle shops make their own noodles, the master skilfully mixing, kneading, rolling and cutting in the front window, tempting customers to duck under the *noren* curtain for a real treat. Fine noodles deserve a fine broth, and house recipes are closely guarded secrets.

...noodle bar

soba noodles with dipping sauce

DIPPING SAUCE
500 ml (2 cups) dashi II (page 245)
125 ml (½ cup) mirin
125 ml (½ cup) Japanese soy sauce
pinch of caster (superfine) sugar

350 g (12 oz) dried soba noodles

CONDIMENTS
nori flakes or strips
spring onions (scallions), thinly sliced
daikon, peeled, finely grated, then
   squeezed to remove excess liquid
wasabi paste
fresh ginger, finely grated

Serves 4 as a light meal

To make the dipping sauce, combine all the ingredients in a bowl and refrigerate for about 30 minutes, or until chilled.

Half-fill a large saucepan with lightly salted water and bring to the boil over high heat, then gradually lower the noodles into the water. Stir so the noodles don't stick together. Add 250 ml (1 cup) cold water and allow it to return to the boil. Repeat this step another two to three times, or until the noodles are tender. This method of cooking is believed to help cook this delicate noodle more evenly. The noodles should be *al dente* with no hard core in the centre but not completely soft all the way through either.

Drain the noodles, then rinse well under cold running water, rubbing the noodles together lightly with your hands to remove any excess starch. Put in a bowl full of water and ice cubes until completely chilled. Drain well and make a neat bundle of noodles on each of four serving plates.

Serve each plate of noodles with an individual bowl of dipping sauce. Using chopsticks, guests mix a little of whichever condiment they desire into their dipping sauce, then dip in a small bundle of the noodles and eat straight away.

2 litres (8 cups) dashi II (page 245)
125 ml (½ cup) Japanese soy sauce
1½ tablespoons caster (superfine) sugar
2 tablespoons mirin
350 g (12 oz) dried soba noodles
2 spring onions (scallions), thinly sliced on
the diagonal
shichimi togarashi (seven spice mix),
to serve, optional

Serves 4 as a light meal

Combine the dashi and ½ teaspoon salt in a saucepan and bring to the boil over high heat. Add the soy sauce, sugar and mirin and stir until the sugar dissolves. Allow the mixture to return to the boil, then reduce to a simmer for 20 minutes.

Meanwhile, half-fill a large saucepan with lightly salted water and bring to the boil over high heat, then gradually lower the noodles into the water. Stir so the noodles don't stick together. Add 250 ml (1 cup) cold water and allow it to return to the boil. Repeat this step another two to three times, or until the noodles are tender. This method of cooking is believed to help cook this delicate noodle more evenly. The noodles should be *al dente* with no hard core in the centre but not completely soft all the way through either.

Drain the noodles, then rinse well under cold running water, rubbing the noodles together lightly with your hands to remove any excess starch.

Divide the noodles among four deep noodle bowls and ladle over the broth. Top with the spring onion and serve immediately. If you like, pass around the shichimi togarashi for sprinkling.

soba noodles in broth

ramen noodles
with soy broth

BROTH
1 kg (2 lb 4 oz) pork bones
1 kg (2 lb 4 oz) chicken bones
10 spring onions (scallions), bruised
10 cm (4 in) piece of fresh ginger, sliced
1 garlic bulb, cut in half through the centre
2 carrots, peeled and chopped
10 cm (4 in) square piece of konbu, wiped
    with a damp cloth
125–185 ml (½–¾ cup) Japanese soy sauce
80 ml (⅓ cup) sake

8 dried shiitake mushrooms
500 g (1 lb 2 oz) fresh ramen noodles
100 g (3½ oz) bamboo shoots, sliced

125 g (4½ oz) Chinese barbecued
    pork, sliced
200 g (7 oz) bok choy (pak choi), sliced
    lengthways into 1.5 cm (⅝ in) wide
    strips, blanched
50 g (1¾ oz) bean sprouts, blanched
4 spring onions (scallions), cut into
    4 cm (1½ in) lengths

CONDIMENTS *(optional)*
nori strips
shichimi togarashi (seven spice mix)
chilli sesame oil

Serves 4 as a main

To make the broth, put the bones in a stockpot or large, deep saucepan and cover with cold water. Bring to the boil over high heat, then drain. Rinse the bones, then return them to a clean stockpot. Add the spring onions, ginger, garlic, carrot and konbu and pour in enough cold water to cover by about 5 cm (2 in). Bring to the boil over high heat, remove the konbu, then reduce to a simmer, skimming any scum off the surface. Cook, uncovered, for 6 hours, or until reduced to about 1.5 litres (6 cups). Cool slightly, remove the bones, then pour the stock through a fine strainer. Refrigerate for 6 hours, or until cold.

Meanwhile, soak the shiitake in hot water for 30 minutes, then drain well. Discard the stems. Bring a large saucepan of lightly salted water to the boil, add the noodles and separate with chopsticks. Cook for 1–2 minutes, or until tender. Drain well, then rinse under cold running water, rubbing the noodles together lightly with your hands to remove any excess starch.

Scoop off any fat from the surface of the cooled broth, then pour the broth into a large saucepan. Add the soy sauce and sake, bring to the boil over high heat, then reduce to a simmer. Pour a little broth into four large warmed bowls, then divide the noodles among the bowls. Ladle broth over the noodles so that it just comes to the top of the noodles. Using chopsticks, neatly arrange small piles of the shiitake, bamboo shoots, pork, bok choy, bean sprouts and spring onion on the noodles. If you wish, serve with the condiments. Freeze any leftover broth for next time.

noodles...

Japan has China to thank for noodles but, like so many imports through the centuries, the Japanese have made them uniquely their own.

Ramen noodles are wheat noodles that are most commonly served in a soy sauce-based broth; however, in Hokkaido a hearty *miso* broth is popular, while in Kyushu a broth cooked from some combination of pork or chicken bones or seafood is favoured. Instant ramen has become popular both in Japan and abroad.

Soba means buckwheat, but is also the name for buckwheat noodles, which is the primary way this grain is utilized in Japan. The natural colour of the soba

noodle is pale to medium brown, although it is sometimes flavoured and coloured with green tea or flecks of citron (yuzu) peel. A popular way to serve the noodles is cold as *zaru soba,* on a bamboo mat or basket-tray, with a dipping sauce called *tsuyu* into which spring onions (scallions) and wasabi are stirred to taste. Soba noodles can also be served in a bowl with a hot broth based on soy sauce ladled over. Known as *kake soba,* there are many variations and any number of toppings, such as *tempura,* deep-fried *tofu,* a dried sardine, or even a raw egg yolk.

Udon, thick white noodles made of wheat, are cooked in quite similar ways to the various kinds of *kake soba.* Though well loved all over the country, *udon* enjoys particular popularity in the area around Osaka.

Somen are wheat noodles too, first lightly oiled and then stretched into the finest strands before drying and packaging. At the height of summer, they are often served in a bowl of iced water garnished with a few slices of cucumber and tomato, and perhaps a prawn (shrimp). *Nagashi somen* is a twist offered by a few speciality restaurants, in which small clumps of the noodles flow down a water channel of bamboo running from kitchen to table, to be snatched up by diners with their chopsticks.

The typically noisy slurping of noodles in Japan often takes visitors aback, but it is not at all impolite. In fact, the air sucked in along with the hot noodles carries some flavourful soup along with with it, and cools everything down to the right temperature.

**2 teaspoons finely chopped dried
  wakame pieces**
500 g (1 lb 2 oz) fresh ramen noodles
**200 g (7 oz) silken firm tofu, cut into
  1.5 cm (⅝ in) cubes**
**2 spring onions (scallions), thinly sliced
  on the diagonal**
1.5 litres (6 cups) dashi II (page 245)
2 tablespoons red miso
1 tablespoon white miso
1 tablespoon mirin
3 teaspoons Japanese soy sauce

Serves 4 as a light meal

Soak the wakame in cold water for 5 minutes, or until rehydrated and glossy but not mushy. Drain well and set aside.

Bring a large saucepan of lightly salted water to the boil, add the noodles and separate with chopsticks. Cook for 1–2 minutes, or until tender. Drain well and rinse under cold water, gently rubbing the noodles to remove any excess starch. Divide the noodles among four deep, warmed bowls. Top with the cubes of tofu and sliced spring onion.

Meanwhile, bring the dashi to the boil in a large saucepan, then reduce to a simmer.

Combine the red and white miso with 250 ml (1 cup) of the dashi stock in a bowl. Whisk until smooth. Return the miso mixture to the saucepan and stir until combined. Allow the liquid to come just to the boil, then add the mirin, soy sauce and wakame and gently heat for 1 minute. Stir, then ladle the broth over the noodles, tofu and spring onion and serve immediately.

miso ramen

nabeyaki udon

4 dried shiitake mushrooms
1 teaspoon sugar
1 litre (4 cups) dashi II (page 245)
150 ml (5 fl oz) Japanese soy sauce
3½ tablespoons mirin
750 g (1 lb 10 oz) fresh udon
noodles
2 chicken thigh fillets, cut into
bite-sized pieces
8 x 5 mm (¼ in) slices of kamaboko
(fish-paste loaf)

2 spring onions (scallions), cut into
5 cm (2 in) lengths
4 eggs
4 tempura prawns (shrimp),
optional (page 92)

CONDIMENTS
ichimi togarashi (chilli powder) or shichimi
togarashi (seven spice mix)

Serves 4 as a light meal

Soak the shiitake in hot water for 30 minutes, then drain well. Discard the stems.
Combine the sugar, 125 ml (½ cup) of the dashi and 1 tablespoon each of
the soy sauce and mirin and bring to the boil. Add the shiitake and cook for
15 minutes, or until the liquid has almost been absorbed. Set the shiitake aside.

Bring a large saucepan of lightly salted water to the boil, add the noodles
and cook for 5 minutes, stirring gently. Drain well and rinse. Divide the
noodles among four 400 ml (14 fl oz) flameproof casserole dishes or
claypots with lids. Combine the remaining dashi, soy sauce and mirin in a
saucepan with ½ teaspoon salt and bring to the boil, then pour over the
noodles so that it just covers them.

Arrange a quarter of the shiitake, chicken, kamaboko and spring onion
on top of the noodles in each dish, keeping each ingredient separate and
leaving some clear space for the egg. Place each dish over medium–high
heat (you may need to do this in batches) and slowly bring to the boil.
Remove any scum that forms on the surface, then reduce to a simmer and cook
for 7 minutes, or until the chicken is just cooked through. Turn off the heat.

Carefully crack an egg into a cup. Using a ladle, press down into the clear
space you left when arranging the other ingredients, to make a hollow, then
carefully slide the raw egg into the hollow without cracking the yolk. Repeat
with the remaining eggs and dishes. Place the lids on top and allow to rest
for 7 minutes, or until the egg is set. If there is a risk of salmonella in your
area, leave on the heat until the egg is completely cooked through. If you
like, serve with a tempura prawn on the side. Pass around the ichimi
togarashi or shichimi togarashi for sprinkling.

1.5 litres (6 cups) dashi II (page 245)
3 spring onions (scallions), two cut into
    4 cm (1½ in) lengths, the other thinly
    sliced on the diagonal
60 ml (¼ cup) mirin
60 ml (¼ cup) Japanese soy sauce
2 teaspoons sugar
400 g (14 oz) fresh udon noodles
shichimi togarashi (seven spice mix),
    to serve, optional

Serves 4 as a light meal

Pour the dashi into a large saucepan and bring to the boil over medium–high heat. Reduce to a simmer.

Add the lengths of spring onion to the dashi along with the mirin, soy sauce and sugar and stir to combine. Simmer over low heat for 5 minutes.

Meanwhile, bring a large saucepan of lightly salted water to the boil, add the noodles and cook, stirring gently, for 5 minutes, or until tender. Drain well and rinse. Divide among four warmed serving bowls. Top with the thinly sliced spring onions. Ladle the liquid over the top. If you like, pass around the shichimi togarashi for sprinkling.

udon noodles in broth

肉うどん

410円

イスセット510円

yakisoba

4 dried shiitake mushrooms
300 g (10½ oz) beef fillet steak or pork
   fillet, thinly sliced across the grain
3 garlic cloves, finely chopped
3 teaspoons finely chopped fresh ginger
500 g (1 lb 2 oz) yakisoba noodles
6 streaky bacon rashers, cut into
   3 cm (1¼ in) squares
2 tablespoons vegetable oil
1 teaspoon sesame oil
6 spring onions (scallions), cut into 3 cm
   (1¼ in) lengths
1 carrot, peeled, thinly sliced on the diagonal
1 small green capsicum (pepper), cut into
   thin strips
250 g (9 oz) Chinese cabbage, thinly sliced
100 g (3½ oz) bamboo shoots, thinly sliced
1 tablespoon thinly sliced pickled ginger

SAUCE
60 ml (¼ cup) Japanese soy sauce
2 tablespoons Worcestershire sauce
1½ tablespoons Japanese rice vinegar
1 tablespoon sake
1 tablespoon mirin
1 tablespoon tomato sauce (ketchup)
1 tablespoon oyster sauce
2 teaspoons lightly crushed black sugar
   or soft brown sugar

CONDIMENTS
pickled ginger
nori flakes or strips, optional
fine katsuobushi (bonito flakes), optional

Serves 4 as a main or 8 as a light meal

Soak the shiitake in hot water for 30 minutes. Drain, reserving 2 tablespoons of the soaking liquid. Discard the stems and thinly slice the caps. Meanwhile, put the beef in a bowl with half the garlic and fresh ginger and mix well. Put the noodles in a colander and pour boiling water over them. Drain and separate.

To make the sauce, combine all the ingredients in a bowl with the reserved mushroom soaking liquid and the remaining garlic and ginger.

Heat a wok over medium–high heat, add the bacon and stir-fry for 3 minutes, or until starting to soften and brown. Set aside in a large bowl. Combine the vegetable and sesame oils in a bowl. Increase the heat to high and add a little of the oil mixture, then stir-fry the beef for 1 minute, or until it starts to change colour all over. Add to the bacon. Add a little more oil to the wok, then stir-fry the shiitake, spring onion, carrot, capsicum, cabbage and bamboo shoots for 1–2 minutes, or until the vegetables are just cooked but still crisp. Add to the bowl with the meat. Add the remaining oil to the wok and stir-fry the noodles for 1 minute. Return the meat and vegetables to the wok, add the sauce and the pickled ginger and stir-fry for 2–3 minutes, or until combined and heated through. Serve immediately, garnished with pickled ginger and, if you like, nori and katsuobushi.

2 Lebanese (short) cucumbers
1 tablespoon dried wakame pieces
100 g (3½ oz) dried somen noodles
12 cooked king prawns (shrimp),
   peeled, deveined and cut in half
   lengthways
3 spring onions (scallions), thinly sliced
   on the diagonal
shichimi togarashi (seven spice mix),
   to serve, optional

DRESSING
½ teaspoon dashi granules
125 ml (½ cup) Japanese rice vinegar
60 ml (¼ cup) mirin
1 teaspoon Japanese soy sauce
2 teaspoons very finely grated
   fresh ginger
pinch of sugar
½ teaspoon sesame oil

Serves 4 as a starter or light meal

Cut the cucumbers in half lengthways, scoop out the seeds with a teaspoon, then slice the flesh very thinly on a slight diagonal. Put the slices of cucumber in a colander, sprinkle with salt and rest for 10 minutes before rinsing and squeezing out as much water as you can. Chill.

Meanwhile, soak the wakame in cold water for 5 minutes, or until rehydrated and glossy but not mushy. Drain well and chill.

To make the dressing, mix the dashi granules with 1 tablespoon hot water until dissolved. Add the rice vinegar, mirin, soy sauce, grated ginger, sugar and sesame oil and stir to combine. Chill.

Bring a large saucepan of water to the boil, then reduce to a simmer. Add the noodles and cook for 2 minutes, or until tender. Quickly drain and rinse under cold running water until completely cool.

Combine the cucumber, wakame, noodles, prawns and half the spring onion in a large bowl. Pour on the dressing and toss well. Serve immediately, garnished with the remaining spring onions and, if you like, sprinkle it with the shichimi togarashi.

somen noodle, prawn and cucumber salad

a little taste of...

An *izakaya* (also called *aka chochin* after the red lantern that typically hangs at the entrance) is a place to sit back and enjoy drinking *sake* in a convivial atmosphere. It is a place where patrons can pause between work and home. *Izakaya* range in styles to suit taste and budget. At their simplest they are the hole-in-the-wall bars with no more than a half-dozen stools and a *mama-san* tending to her regulars with a house *sake* and a few home-cooked tidbits. Then there are larger, more stylish establishments offering dozens of quality regional *sake* from remote corners of the archipelago and many small, tasty dishes to accompany it. The best invariably offer a homey and intimate atmosphere, and the owner takes pride in knowing the regular customers, remembering their favourite brand of *sake,* and recommending others to suit their taste. The dim and smoky atmosphere (smoke from cigarettes as well as from the grill) of *izakaya* has traditionally been restricted to men. But today they are also frequented by couples and working women, and many now cater to the growing number of female customers by providing comfortable surroundings to suit them.

...izakaya

fresh soya
beans in the pod

**500 g (1 lb 2 oz) fresh or frozen soya
beans in pods**
**1 litre (4 cups) dashi I (page 245),
optional**
3 teaspoons salt

Serves 4–6 as a snack

Rub the fresh soya beans with salt between your hands to rub off the fine hairy fibres. Rinse the pods. If you are using frozen soya beans, this step is not necessary.

Pour the dashi and 250 ml (1 cup) water, or 1.25 litres (5 cups) water into a saucepan and bring to the boil over high heat. Add the soya beans and cook for 6–8 minutes if using fresh or 3–4 minutes if using frozen, or until tender but still bright green. Drain. You can serve these either warm, at room temperature or chilled.

Sprinkle with salt. To eat, simply suck the beans out of the pods and throw the pods away. Supply a bowl to collect the empty pods.

FILLING
200 g (7 oz) Chinese cabbage, stems
   removed, finely chopped
200 g (7 oz) minced (ground) pork
2 teaspoons finely grated fresh ginger
3 garlic cloves, crushed
1½ tablespoons Japanese soy sauce
2 teaspoons sake
2 teaspoons mirin
¼ teaspoon ground white pepper
2 spring onions (scallions),
   finely chopped

DIPPING SAUCE
80 ml (⅓ cup) Japanese rice vinegar
80 ml (⅓ cup) Japanese soy sauce
2 teaspoons sesame oil or chilli sesame oil

200 g (7 oz) packet gyoza wrappers
vegetable oil, for pan-frying, plus
   an extra 2 teaspoons
2 teaspoons sesame oil
Japanese mustard, to serve, optional

Makes 30

To make the filling, put the cabbage in a colander, sprinkle with salt and stand for 30 minutes. Squeeze well, then mix with the rest of the filling ingredients.

Meanwhile, to make the dipping sauce, put all the ingredients in a small bowl and stir to combine. Divide among small sauce dishes.

Lay a wrapper in the palm of your hand and put 2 teaspoons of the filling in the middle. Lightly dampen the edge of the wrapper with water, then fold the edges together to form a semicircle, pressing firmly to enclose the filling. Lightly dampen the curved edge of the wrapper, then overlap around the edge to form a pleat. Put each dumpling on a tray lined with plastic wrap. Repeat with the remaining wrappers and filling. Refrigerate until ready to cook.

Heat a little oil in a large, non-stick frying pan over medium–high heat. Put the dumpling in the pan, flat-side down, in a single layer, leaving a little space between each dumpling. (If your pan is not large enough to fit all the dumplings at once, cook them in batches.) Cook for 2 minutes, or until the bottoms are crisp and golden. Combine 125 ml (½ cup) boiling water with 2 teaspoons of the vegetable oil and the sesame oil, then add to the pan. Cover, reduce the heat to low and cook for about 10 minutes. Remove the lid, increase the heat to high and cook until the liquid has evaporated, making sure the dumplings don't catch and burn. Remove from the pan and drain on paper towels. Serve with the dipping sauce.

pork dumplings

japanese
spring rolls

DIPPING SAUCE
60 ml (¼ cup) tamari or Japanese soy sauce
1½ tablespoons Japanese rice vinegar
1 tablespoon mirin
1 teaspoon caster (superfine) sugar

FILLING
90 g (3¼ oz) Chinese cabbage, finely
   shredded
3 dried shiitake mushrooms
30 g (1 oz) harusame (bean thread noodles)
200 g (7 oz) minced (ground) pork
90 g (3¼ oz) bamboo shoots, finely chopped
4 spring onions (scallions), finely chopped

1 tablespoon finely grated fresh ginger
1 garlic clove, crushed
1½ tablespoons sake
1½ tablespoons Japanese soy sauce
1 tablespoon mirin
1 teaspoon sesame oil
large pinch of ground white pepper
2 tablespoons potato starch

1 tablespoon potato starch, extra
12 x 18 cm (7 in) spring roll wrappers
vegetable oil, for deep-frying

Makes 12

To make the dipping sauce, combine all the ingredients in a small bowl and stir until the sugar has dissolved.

To make the filling, put the cabbage in a colander. Sprinkle with salt and stand for 30 minutes, then squeeze well. Meanwhile, soak the shiitake in hot water for 30 minutes. Drain, discard the stems and thinly slice the caps. Soak the harusame in warm water for 10 minutes. Drain, squeeze out any excess moisture, then roughly chop. Put the cabbage, shiitake and noodles in a large bowl with the rest of the filling ingredients except the potato starch and mix well. Add the potato starch and mix again. Season with salt.

Combine the extra potato starch with enough cold water to form a thin paste. Lay a spring roll wrapper on a workbench with a corner facing you. Put 1 heaped tablespoon of the filling in a sausage shape across the wrapper, about 2 cm (¾ in) up from the bottom corner. Fold the bottom corner up and roll up, folding the sides in as you go. Seal the edge with a little of the potato paste. Set aside and continue with the remaining wrappers and mixture.

Fill a deep-fat fryer or large saucepan one-third full of oil and heat to 170°C (325°F), or until a cube of bread dropped into the oil browns in 20 seconds. Fry the spring rolls a few at a time for 10 minutes, or until golden and cooked through. Drain on paper towels and keep warm in a low oven while you cook the rest. Serve immediately with the dipping sauce.

yakitori bar

Yaki means roasted or grilled, and *tori* means bird, fowl or chicken. Imperial records show that *yakitori* was among the foods served at a court feast in Kyoto in 1587. In those early days the *tori* would have been wild birds such as ducks, quails or pigeons. Seventeenth-century farmers travelling on foot to worship the rice god at Kyoto's Shinto shrine, Fushimi Inari Taisha, are said to have popularized this simple food by skewering and roasting sparrows, the bane of the paddies, to eat along their way. Sparrows are still served at *yakitori-ya* near the shrine gate.

In the Yurakucho district of Tokyo, a favourite salaryman haunt is 'under the tracks' where every evening makeshift open-air food stalls offer succulent grilled tidbits of chicken and vegetables, along with chicken livers, hearts, intestines, skin and even cartilage to their sake- and beer-drinking clientele. Upmarket chefs in more elegant surroundings, on the other hand, might fill their skewers with such delicacies as duck breast basted with balsamic vinegar, shiitake stuffed with ground (minced) ginger chicken, or pork rolled with shiso leaves.

SAUCE
500 g (1 lb 2 oz) chicken wings, cut into
   3 pieces at the joints
375 ml (1½ cups) mirin
250 ml (1 cup) sake
375 ml (1½ cups) Japanese soy sauce
55 g (¼ cup) caster (superfine) sugar
3 teaspoons kuzu starch rocks or arrowroot

500 g (1 lb 2 oz) large chicken thigh fillets
4 baby leeks or thick spring onions
   (scallions), white part only, cut into four

Makes 8

Soak eight small bamboo skewers in water for 1 hour.

To make the sauce, preheat the griller (broiler) to high. Cook the chicken wings, turning occasionally, for 15 minutes, or until dark golden and starting to blacken slightly. Remove and set aside. Pour the mirin and sake into a saucepan over high heat and bring to the boil. Add the soy sauce and sugar and stir until the sugar is dissolved. Add the wings and bring the liquid to the boil, then reduce to a simmer for 30 minutes. Remove the pan from the heat and allow to cool for 30 minutes. Strain the sauce (you can serve the chicken wings as a snack). Pour a little of the sauce into a small dish and add the kuzu. Crush the rocks and stir into the liquid until it has dissolved, then return to the pan. Put the pan over high heat and stir until the mixture boils and becomes thick and glossy. Remove from the heat and allow to cool before using.

Cut each thigh fillet into 12 even pieces. Starting with a piece of chicken and alternating with leek, thread 3 pieces of chicken and 2 pieces of leek onto each skewer. Pour a little of the sauce into a small dish for basting and reserve the rest for serving.

Heat a griller to high and cook the skewers, turning regularly, for 3–4 minutes, then baste with the sauce. Cook on each side for a further 1–2 minutes, basting again during this time, until well glazed and the chicken is cooked through. Serve with a drizzle of the sauce.

地下鉄
SUBWAY

銀座線
Ginza Line

yakitori

agedashi
tofu

600 g (1 lb 5 oz) block silken firm tofu
vegetable oil, for deep-frying
60 ml (¼ cup) sesame oil, optional
katakuriko or potato starch, for coating
70 g (2½ oz) daikon, peeled, finely grated,
 then squeezed to remove excess liquid
2 teaspoons finely grated fresh ginger

SAUCE
170 ml (⅔ cup) dashi II (page 245)
2 tablespoons Japanese soy sauce
1 tablespoon sake
1 tablespoon mirin

GARNISH
fine katsuobushi (bonito flakes)
nori flakes or strips
thinly sliced spring onion (scallion)

Serves 4 as a starter

Be very careful when working with the tofu—it is very soft and breaks easily. To weight the tofu, wrap it in a clean tea towel. Put two plates on top of the tofu and leave for about 30 minutes to extract any excess moisture. Remove from the tea towel, cut into eight pieces, then pat dry with paper towels.

To make the sauce, combine all the ingredients in a small saucepan and bring to the boil over high heat, then reduce the heat to very low to keep the sauce warm until ready to use.

Fill a deep-fat fryer or large saucepan one-third full of vegetable oil, then add the sesame oil, if using. Heat to 180°C (350°F), or until a cube of bread dropped into the oil browns in 15 seconds.

Lightly coat the tofu with the katakuriko and deep-fry in batches for about 3 minutes, or until it just starts to become a pale golden colour around the edges. Drain well on paper towels, then divide among four individual (or one large, wide) bowls and carefully pour the sauce into the base. Top the tofu with a little daikon and ginger. Garnish with the katsuobushi, nori or spring onion as desired. Eat with chopsticks and, if you need one, a spoon.

WASABI MAYONNAISE DIPPING SAUCE
125 g (½ cup) Japanese mayonnaise
1 teaspoon Japanese soy sauce
1 teaspoon mirin
1 teaspoon Japanese rice vinegar
½ teaspoon wasabi paste

SALMON AND TOFU BALLS
200 g (7 oz) silken firm tofu
400 g (14 oz) tinned red salmon, well
   drained to yield about 250 g (9 oz)
2 spring onions (scallions), finely chopped
2 teaspoons finely grated fresh ginger,
   squeezed to remove excess liquid

1 garlic clove, crushed
2 teaspoons mirin
1 tablespoon Japanese soy sauce
1 egg
2 tablespoons plain (all-purpose) flour
pinch of ground white pepper

potato starch, for coating
vegetable oil, for deep-frying
lemon wedges, to serve

Makes 18

To make the dipping sauce, put all the ingredients in a small bowl and combine well.

To weight the tofu, wrap it in a clean tea towel. Put two plates on top of the tofu and leave for about 2 hours to extract any excess moisture. Remove from the tea towel, then pat dry with paper towels. Put in a bowl and finely mash with a fork. Break up the salmon with a fork, picking out any bones. Finely mash with a fork and add to the bowl with the tofu, along with the spring onion, ginger, garlic, mirin, soy sauce, egg and flour and combine well. Season with salt and white pepper. If the mixture is still too wet, then put in a fine colander and leave for 30 minutes to drain out any excess liquid. With clean hands, form into balls about the size of a walnut and set aside— you should get about 18 balls. Don't worry if the balls seem quite soft.

Fill a deep-fat fryer or large saucepan one-third full of oil and heat to 180°C (350°F), or until a cube of bread dropped into the oil browns in 15 seconds. Lightly coat the balls in potato starch then immediately lower into the oil. Cook in batches, turning occasionally, for 2–3 minutes, or until golden all over and cooked through. Drain on paper towels and keep warm in a low oven while you repeat with the remaining mixture. Serve immediately with lemon wedges and the wasabi mayonnaise dipping sauce.

salmon and
tofu balls

sake

To the people of ancient Japan, the natural fermentation of rice seemed a mysterious and magical phenomenon, and the resulting intoxicating beverage was long limited to sacred use. Today, of course, the process is a science and *sake* is considered the perfect brew to accompany Japanese food. Despite the fact that *sake* is now so common, it maintains its ceremonial importance as an essential offering to the Shinto deities, as well as the ritual solemnizer at Shinto weddings.

Sake is the most Japanese of drinks. It often plays a part in traditional celebrations of nature; for instance it is imbibed beneath blossoming cherry trees during the spring

o-hanami, flower viewing, and winter *yukimi,* snow viewing. Small cups of *sake* are sometimes sipped from floating trays in outdoor hot spring baths during the winter season. For a joyous occasion *sake* containing tiny flakes of real gold may be poured, and at certain festive times, shrines and temples serve a milder sweet version, *ama-zake,* which even children are welcome to enjoy.

Since the eighth century it has been customary to heat *sake* in winter. This custom not only warms body and soul, but also helps to improve the flavour of lower quality *sake.* However, the best are most delicious when served at room temperature or chilled.

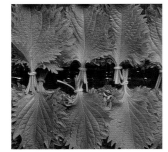

rare beef with condiments

vegetable oil, for pan-frying
2 x 200 g (7 oz) beef fillet steaks
1 quantity ponzu (page 246) or
    250 ml (1 cup) ready-made ponzu

CONDIMENTS
70 g (2½ oz) daikon, peeled, finely grated,
    then sqeezed to remove excess liquid
2 teaspoons finely grated fresh ginger
1 tablespoon very finely julienned
    shiso leaves
wasabi paste

Serves 4 as a starter

Heat a little of the oil in a heavy-based frying pan over high heat. Season the beef with salt and pepper and cook for 5–7 minutes, or until well browned all over before plunging quickly into iced water to stop the cooking process. Remove from the water and pat dry with a clean tea towel. The beef should be very rare.

Slice the meat very thinly, then neatly lay the slices onto four individual serving plates. Accompany each serve with a small bowl of ponzu for dipping and small mounds of condiments. Using chopsticks, each guest mixes the condiments into the sauce, adjusting the flavour as desired. Dip the slices of beef into the sauce before eating.

1 kg (2 lb 4 oz) chicken thigh cutlets
   or fillets, skin on
60 ml (¼ cup) Japanese soy sauce
60 ml (¼ cup) mirin
1 tablespoon sake
2 teaspoons finely grated fresh ginger
   and its juice
3 garlic cloves, crushed
katakuriko or potato starch, for coating
oil, for deep-frying
lemon wedges, to serve

Serves 6–8 as a snack

Remove the bone from the cutlets and cut the chicken into 4 cm (1½ in)
squares. Combine the soy sauce, mirin, sake, ginger and juice, and garlic
in a non-metallic bowl and add the chicken. Stir to coat, cover with plastic
wrap and marinate in the fridge for 1 hour.

Fill a deep-fat fryer or large saucepan one-third full of oil and heat to
180°C (350°F), or until a cube of bread dropped into the oil browns in
15 seconds.

Drain the chicken pieces well, discarding the marinade. Lightly coat the
chicken in the katakuriko and shake off any excess. Deep-fry in batches for
6–7 minutes, or until golden and crisp and the chicken is just cooked through.
Drain well on paper towels and sprinkle with salt. Serve with lemon wedges.

deep-fried
marinated chicken

tofu dengaku

700 g (1 lb 9 oz) firm (cotton) tofu
100 g (⅓ cup) red or white miso
1 egg yolk
1½ tablespoons dashi II (page 245)
2 teaspoons mirin
2 teaspoons sugar
vegetable oil, for brushing

GARNISH *(optional)*
nori flakes
thinly sliced spring onion
  (scallion)
lightly toasted sesame seeds

Serves 4–6 as a starter

To weight the tofu, wrap it in a clean tea towel. Sit two plates on top of the tofu to extract any excess moisture and leave it for about 1 hour, or until the tofu is about half its original thickness. Remove from the tea towel, then pat dry with paper towels.

Meanwhile, combine the miso, egg yolk, dashi, mirin and sugar in a bowl and whisk until smooth.

Preheat the griller (broiler) to high. Cut the tofu into six even slices and put on a foil-lined tray. Lightly brush the tofu blocks with a little vegetable oil and put under the griller for 2–3 minutes, or until lightly golden. Turn and repeat on the other side.

Thickly spread the miso mixture onto one side of the tofu and sit under the griller again, miso-side up, for a few minutes, or until bubbling and golden in places. Serve immediately, sprinkled with one or a mixture of the suggested garnishes, if you like.

SKEWERS
8 small scallops, roe removed
4 raw medium prawns (shrimp), peeled
   and deveined, tails intact
225 g (8 oz) pork fillet, cut into
   3 x 2 cm (1¼ x ¾ in) pieces about
   1 cm (½ in) thick
spring onion (scallion), cut into 3 cm
   (1¼ in) lengths
4 x 5 mm (¼ in) thick, small slices of
   jap pumpkin, unpeeled
225 g (8 oz) beef fillet, cut into
   3 x 2 cm (1¼ x ¾ in) pieces about
   1 cm (½ in) thick
175 g (6 oz) firm fish fillet (e.g. snapper,
   salmon, tuna or swordfish), cut into
   3 x 2 cm (1¼ x ¾ in) pieces

pinch of ground white pepper
plain (all-purpose) flour, for dusting
lightly beaten egg, for coating
panko (Japanese breadcrumbs), for coating
vegetable oil, for deep-frying
60 ml (¼ cup) sesame oil, optional

CONDIMENTS
1 quantity tonkatsu sauce (page 201)
lemon wedges
Japanese mustard
crisp English cabbage leaves, cut into
   3 x 2 cm (1¼ x ¾ in) squares

Serves 4 as a starter

Soak 24 bamboo skewers in water for 1 hour.

Use four skewers for each group of ingredients. Use the following list as a guide to what should go on each skewer: 2 scallops; 1 prawn threaded lengthways so the tail is at the top of the skewer; alternating pieces of pork (3 pieces) and spring onion (2 pieces); 1 piece of pumpkin; 3 pieces of beef; 3 pieces of fish.

Lightly season each skewer with salt and white pepper, then dip into the flour, shaking off any excess. Dip into the beaten egg, allowing any excess to drip off, then press into the crumbs to coat well. Refrigerate until needed.

Fill a deep-fat fryer or large saucepan half full with the vegetable oil and sesame oil, if using, and heat to 170°C (325°F), or until a cube of bread dropped into the oil browns in 20 seconds. Cooking a few skewers at a time, lower them into the oil and cook until golden and crisp. The cooking time will vary with each ingredient but should take 1–3 minutes. Drain well on paper towels.

Serve with tonkatsu sauce, lemon wedges, mustard and a small bowl of the cabbage. For a more substantial meal, serve with rice, miso soup and pickles.

crumbed skewers

savoury
japanese custard

625 ml (2½ cups) dashi II (page 245)
1 chicken thigh fillet (about 150 g/5½ oz),
   cut into 1.5 cm (⅝ in) pieces
4 raw medium prawns (shrimp), peeled
   and deveined
4 eggs
3 teaspoons Japanese soy sauce
2 teaspoons mirin

2 teaspoons sake
4 small fresh shiitake mushrooms, stems
   discarded, caps quartered
1 spring onion (scallion), sliced on
   the diagonal
1 tablespoon ginkgo nuts, optional

Serves 4 as a starter

Bring the dashi to the boil in a small saucepan over high heat. Reduce to a simmer, then add the chicken and prawns and poach for 30 seconds, or until the prawns are just turning pink and curling. Remove with a slotted spoon and allow the dashi to cool to room temperature.

Put the eggs in a bowl and lightly beat.

Add the soy sauce, mirin, sake and a pinch of salt to the dashi. Pour the mixture into the egg—stir but do not beat as this will form too many air bubbles. Strain the mixture through a fine sieve.

Fill a large saucepan (it needs to be large enough to fit a bamboo steamer on top) with water and bring to the boil over high heat, then reduce to a simmer.

Divide the chicken, prawns, shiitake, spring onion and ginkgo (if using) among four *chawan mushi* cups with lids, or 375 ml (1½ cup) bowls. Ladle the egg mixture over the top, stopping about 2 cm (¾ in) from the top of the cup—you should have some egg mixture leftover. Put the cups (without lids) in a large bamboo steamer.

Wrap a clean tea towel around the steamer lid and put the lid on, wedging a bamboo skewer between the steamer and the lid to allow some of the steam to escape. Sit the steamer over the pan of simmering water and steam for about 18 minutes, or until the egg is just set. Top up each cup with about 1 cm (½ in) more of the egg mixture and cook for a further 2–3 minutes, or until set.

If you have lids for your cups, put them on to keep the custard warm. Serve with a small spoon to eat the custard and chopsticks to eat the solids.

600 g (1 lb 5 oz) block silken firm tofu, chilled
1 tablespoon finely grated fresh ginger and its juice
2 spring onions (scallions), thinly sliced
2 teaspoons white or black sesame seeds, toasted
finely shredded shiso leaves, optional
fine katsuobushi (bonito flakes), for sprinkling, optional
Japanese soy sauce, for drizzling
sesame oil or chilli sesame oil, for drizzling

Serves 4 as a starter

Be very careful when working with the tofu—it is very soft and breaks easily. Cut the tofu into quarters, then put one piece of tofu in each of four small serving bowls.

Top each serving with a little grated fresh ginger and juice, some spring onion and sesame seeds. If you like, sprinkle the tofu with shredded shiso leaves and katsuobushi. Drizzle with a little soy sauce and sesame oil, then serve immediately.

chilled tofu with ginger and spring onion

a little taste of...

Tokyo's vast central wholesale market at Tsukiji is a world of its own. Nearly 3,000 tonnes of fish pass through it each market day, which works out at some 900,000 tonnes per year. The day starts early, as workers bow at the entrance of Namiyoke Jinja, the 'Wave-calming Shrine', by the market gate. Fishing boats dock at the pier and trucks roll in through the dark hours, delivering the fresh seafood catch from Japan's fishing ports, as well as air cargo from around the world. The largest and most celebrated of the market's products, frozen tunas, are inspected and readied for the day's auction. Near dawn, auctioneers and bidders begin their frenzied rounds of shouting and hand signals, completely unintelligible to the uninitiated, closing a sale every few seconds. Restaurateurs, middlemen and retailers make their daily selection from the hundreds of stalls that together offer more than 400 varieties of seafood. A good morning's work behind them, by 8 o'clock buyers and sellers are ready for breakfast at one of the market restaurants — the freshest sushi on earth.

...fish market

crab, cucumber and wakame salad

2 Lebanese (short) cucumbers
2 tablespoons dried wakame pieces
150 g (5½ oz) fresh, cooked crabmeat,
    picked over (or good-quality tinned
    crabmeat)

DRESSING
2 tablespoons Japanese rice vinegar
2 tablespoons dashi II (page 245)
1 tablespoon Japanese soy sauce
2 teaspoons mirin
1½ teaspoons ginger juice (page 247)

Serves 4 as a starter

Dissolve 2 teaspoons of salt in 500 ml (2 cups) cold water. Cut the cucumbers in half lengthways, scoop out the seeds, then slice the flesh very thinly. Put the cucumber flesh in the cold water and soak for 10 minutes. Drain well and gently squeeze out any excess moisture. Keep in the refrigerator until needed.

Soak the wakame in a bowl of cold water for 5 minutes, or until rehydrated and glossy but not mushy. Drain well, then refrigerate until needed.

Make the dressing by combining the rice vinegar, dashi, soy sauce and mirin in a small saucepan and bring to the boil over high heat. Remove from the heat and cool to room temperature. Add the ginger juice to the dressing and stir well. Allow to cool completely. Refrigerate for 15 minutes until cold.

Neatly arrange the cucumber, wakame and crabmeat into four small serving dishes, then carefully pour the dressing over the top.

8 snow peas (mangetout), very thinly
   sliced on the diagonal
½ carrot, peeled, very finely julienned
8 large or 12 small scallops, roe removed
1 litre (4 cups) dashi I (page 245)
1 teaspoon Japanese soy sauce
1 teaspoon mirin
4 thin strips of lemon zest
4 mitsuba leaves or small shiso leaves,
   optional

Serves 4 as a starter

Bring a small saucepan of water to the boil over high heat, then reduce to
a simmer. Add the snow peas for a few seconds, then remove with a slotted
spoon and plunge into iced water. Add the carrot and cook for 30 seconds,
then remove with a slotted spoon and plunge into iced water.

Add the scallops to the simmering water and cook for 1 minute, then lift out
and drain well. Neatly place a small bundle each of the snow pea strips
and julienned carrot into the base of four small soup bowls, then put the
scallops on top.

Pour the dashi, soy sauce and mirin into a small saucepan and bring to the
boil over high heat, then reduce to a simmer.

Tie each lemon strip into a knot or loop and add one to each bowl. Carefully
ladle the dashi broth into the soup bowls then float a mitsuba leaf on top.
Serve immediately.

clear soup
with scallops

salt-grilled fish

vegetable oil
4 x 175–200 g (6–7 oz) fish fillets,
  skin on, or 2 small whole fish
1–2 teaspoons salt
lemon wedges, for serving

Serves 4 as a main

If you are using long thin fish fillets, soak eight bamboo skewers in water for 1 hour.

Lightly oil a wire rack. Slash the flesh side of the fillets a few times to prevent them curling. Sprinkle the fish liberally with salt on both sides and sit, skin-side up, on the oiled rack with a dish underneath to catch any drips. Leave it for 5–10 minutes if using a white fleshed fish, about 30 minutes if using an oilier and thicker fish fillet such as salmon or tuna, and up to 50 minutes if using a whole fish.

If you are using long thin fish fillets, run two bamboo skewers through the width of the fillets to prevent the fish from curling up too much.

Preheat the griller (broiler) to high. Lift the wire rack onto a baking tray. Sit under the griller and adjust the grill plate so the fish is about 8 cm (3 in) from the heat source. Cook the fish for 4–6 minutes, or until the skin is starting to colour and puff up slightly. Carefully turn over and cook for 1–2 minutes on the other side, or until just cooked through and opaque. The length of time to cook the fish will vary depending on the thickness of the fillet. Whole fish may take around 5 minutes per side. If you have skewers through the fish to hold its shape, you may need to turn the skewers a few times to prevent the flesh from sticking to them, so that they can be easily removed before serving. Serve with the lemon wedges and some rice.

20 raw large prawns (shrimp)
30 g (¼ cup) plain (all-purpose) flour,
    for coating
¼ teaspoon ground white pepper
1 egg
60 g (1 cup) panko (Japanese
    breadcrumbs)
vegetable oil, for deep-frying
60 ml (¼ cup) sesame oil
lemon wedges, to serve

DIPPING SAUCE
170 g (⅔ cup) Japanese mayonnaise
1½ tablespoons finely chopped pickled
    Japanese cucumber or dill pickles
1 tablespoon Japanese rice vinegar
1 spring onion (scallion), white part only,
    finely chopped
7 g (¼ cup) chopped mitsuba leaves
1 garlic clove, crushed
pinch of ground white pepper

Serves 4 as a starter

Peel and devein the prawns, leaving the tails intact. Make three cuts in the belly of the prawns. Turn the prawns over and, starting from the tail end, press down gently at intervals along the length of the prawn—this helps to break the connective tissue, preventing the prawns from curling up too much.

Season the flour with white pepper and ¼ teaspoon salt. Break the egg into a bowl, add 2 teaspoons water and lightly beat together. Holding the prawns by their tails so the tails remain uncoated, coat them lightly in flour, then into the egg, allowing any excess to drip off. Finally, coat with the panko, pressing on to help adhere. Refrigerate until you are ready to cook.

To make the dipping sauce, put all the ingredients in a small bowl and stir to combine. Season to taste with salt and white pepper. Refrigerate until ready to serve.

Fill a deep-fat fryer or large saucepan one-third full of vegetable oil and add the sesame oil. Heat to 180°C (350°F), or until a cube of bread dropped into the oil browns in 15 seconds. Deep-fry the prawns in batches for 2 minutes, or until golden. Drain on paper towels and serve immediately accompanied by the dipping sauce and lemon wedges.

deep-fried prawns
with dipping sauce

sushi bar... The origins of sushi lie in the ancient Asian custom of preserving raw fish in fermenting rice, and such *nare-zushi* can still be eaten in a few remote Japanese villages, though to outsiders the taste is considered unappealing when compared to modern-day sushi.

The sushi that is familiar to us today, a slice of raw fish atop a ball of lightly vinegared rice, is a product of late seventeenth century Edo (old Tokyo). This traditional sushi is called *Edomae-zushi*—in-front-of-Edo sushi—after the bay at the city's feet. Right up until the 1950s it was sold not in shops, but rather by roving street peddlers who carried their goods in boxes carefully balanced on poles across their shoulders.

Sushi has became ever more popular, spreading to other parts of Japan and, eventually, to the world. Ironically, in the last few years chic shops specializing in the 'New York' or 'California' style sushi have popped up around Tokyo, re-importing sushi as it has been transformed abroad.

In Japan, a sushi chef has likely devoted 10 years to apprenticeship, having spent the first four observing the master and performing basic and peripheral chores before ever wielding a knife on fish. Watching him (for it is almost always a man) is a great show, as every precise cut and gesture has been perfected by endless repetition.

The key elements a Japanese patron looks for in a favourite *sushi-ya* — sushi bar — are fresh fish, delicious rice and a simple, home-like atmosphere. The sushi master will banter with his guests and on a great night, with the help of beer or *sake,* the people around the bar might come together like a family.

Kaiten-zushi is sushi on a conveyor-belt. Busy people pop in for a few bites and some tea. They stack up their empty plates and the bill is reckoned from the plate count. Sometimes called *kuru-kuru-zushi* for it just keeps 'coming-coming', this is quick, cheap and fun, but of course can never reach the sublime levels of the more upscale sushi experience.

hand-moulded sushi

10 cooked prawns (shrimp)
1 tablespoon Japanese rice vinegar
½ quantity prepared sushi rice (page 244)
10 sashimi slices (page 86)
wasabi paste, for spreading

CONDIMENTS
Japanese soy sauce
wasabi paste, optional
pickled ginger, optional

Makes 20

Peel the prawns, then slit them along their bellies, ensuring you don't cut through to the other side. Carefully remove the intestinal tract.

Fill a bowl with warm water and mix in the rice vinegar. Dampen your hands with the vinegared water to prevent the rice sticking to your hands. Form a slightly heaped tablespoon of rice into a rounded rectangle about 5 x 2 cm (2 x ¾ in), wetting your hands as needed. Put on a tray lined with plastic wrap, then cover with a damp tea towel. Repeat with the remaining rice—you should get about 20 mounds.

Put a slice of sashimi on the palm of your left hand, then use a finger on your right hand to smear a little wasabi paste over the top. Put a piece of the moulded rice along the fish, and gently cup your left palm to make a slight curve, then using the middle and index fingers of your right hand, press the rice onto the fish, firmly pushing with a slight downward motion, keeping the shape as neat and compact as possible. Turn the fish over so it is facing upwards then neaten up the shape, keeping your left hand flat. Put rice-side down on a plate and cover with plastic wrap while you repeat with the rest of the fish. Repeat the same process with the prawns, which should have the belly side against the rice.

Serve with a small bowl of soy sauce for dipping into, and, if desired, a little extra wasabi paste on the side to mix into the sauce and some pickled ginger as a palate refresher. Eat with your fingers and dip the fish side into the dipping sauce, not the rice side.

1 tablespoon Japanese rice vinegar
4 toasted nori sheets
1 quantity prepared sushi rice (page 244)
wasabi paste, for spreading

FILLING
60 g (2¼ oz) prepared kanpyo
   (gourd strip)
100 g (3½ oz) firm tofu, cut into
   long strips about 1 cm (½ in) thick
   and wide

85 g (3 oz) simmered shiitake mushrooms,
   thinly sliced (page 136)
100 g (3½ oz) takuan (pickled daikon), cut
   into 1 cm (½ in) thick strips

CONDIMENTS
Japanese soy sauce
wasabi paste, optional
pickled ginger, optional

Makes 4 thick rolls or 24 thick pieces

Fill a bowl with warm water and mix in the rice vinegar. Lay a sheet of nori, shiny-side down, on a bamboo mat with the short end of the mat towards you. Dampen your hands with the vinegared water to prevent the rice sticking to your hands. Starting at the edge nearest to you and stopping about 5 cm (2 in) from the edge furthest from you, spread about 250 g (1½ cups) prepared sushi rice over the nori, pressing down with your fingers—it should be about 1 cm (½ in) thick. Wet your hands as needed.

About 8 cm (3 in) in from the end closest to you, use your finger to smear a little wasabi paste along the width of the roll. Take one type of filling at a time and lay it along the wasabi paste from end to end so that you have a long strip across the rice. Repeat with the other ingredients, each one snugly on top of and next to the other, then trim the edges.

Holding the filling in place with the tips of your fingers, lift the closest end of the bamboo mat with your thumbs and, holding everything taut, roll the sushi away from you, making sure you do not tuck the edge of the mat under the roll. When the roll is finished, press the mat down over the top to form a neat, firm roll. Unroll the mat and put the sushi roll, seam-side down, on a cutting board. Repeat with the remaining ingredients to make four rolls.

Using a very sharp, large knife, trim the ends of each roll. Dipping the knife into water as you slice to prevent the rice from sticking to it, cut each roll into six to eight even pieces. Arrange cut-side up on a platter.

Serve with a small bowl of soy sauce for dipping into, and, if desired, extra wasabi to mix into the sauce and some pickled ginger as a palate refresher.

rolled sushi

pressed sushi

16 cooked king prawns (shrimp)
2 tablespoons Japanese rice vinegar
1 teaspoon caster (superfine) sugar
wasabi paste, optional
1 tablespoon Japanese rice vinegar, extra
1 quantity prepared sushi rice (page 244)
125 g (4½ oz) flying fish roe or salmon roe
4 toasted nori sheets

Makes 16 pieces

Line a 26 x 16 cm (10½ x 6½ in) baking tin about 4 cm (1½ in) deep with two long pieces of plastic wrap so that it overhangs on all sides. You will also need another slightly smaller tin or dish.

Peel the prawns, then slit them along their bellies, ensuring you don't cut all the way through. Carefully remove the vein. Mix the vinegar with the sugar and a pinch of salt until the sugar is dissolved, then add the prawns and mix. Set aside for 15 minutes. Drain well, then neatly and snugly arrange the prawns in a single layer, belly-side up, in the baking tin. Flatten with your hands then smear a little wasabi over the cut side of each prawn, if you are using it.

Fill a bowl with warm water and mix in the extra rice vinegar. Dampen your hands with the water to prevent the rice sticking to your hands. Carefully spread half the rice over the prawns, without moving the prawns, then press down firmly. Smooth the rice over so that it forms an even layer, wetting your hands as needed.

Spead the roe over the rice in a thin even layer with the back of a spoon, then press down gently. Trim two sheets of the nori to fit the tin and cover the rice in a single layer. Press down to adhere. Add the second half of the rice, pressing and smoothing as you did earlier, then trim the remaining two sheets of nori to cover the rice and press down again to adhere.

Fold the plastic wrap over the sides to enclose the rice. Put the smaller tin on top of the plastic and fill with cold water to weigh down the sushi. Leave for 30 minutes, then remove. Unfold the plastic wrap and invert the sushi onto a platter. Remove the plastic wrap carefully so the prawns stay in place. Use a knife to cut into 16 rectangles, each containing a prawn.

1 quantity prepared sushi rice
   (page 244)
10 toasted nori sheets
Japanese soy sauce, for serving
wasabi paste, to serve
pickled ginger, to serve
1 tablespoon Japanese rice vinegar

FILLINGS
175 g (6 oz) tin crabmeat, drained
2 tablespoons Japanese mayonnaise
1 Lebanese (short) cucumber, cut in half,
   then into long, thin strips
1 avocado, thinly sliced
100 g (3½ oz) smoked salmon,
   cut into strips

Makes 20

Put the sushi rice into a serving dish. Using scissors or a very sharp knife, cut each nori sheet in half.

Combine the crabmeat with the mayonnaise, then heap it neatly on a platter. Arrange the other fillings on the same platter. Put the rice, nori, fillings, soy sauce, wasabi paste and pickled ginger in the centre of the dining table for each person to make their own sushi. Add a little rice vinegar to bowls of warm water and put these on the table—by dampening your hands in the vinegared water you will prevent the rice from sticking to your hands.

To roll the sushi, put the rectangle of nori on your left palm. Take a heaped tablespoon of rice and form it into a rough oblong, then put it in the centre, just slightly towards the left edge of the nori. Add one or several of the fillings along the length of the rice, being careful not to add too much or the rolls will split, then roll up into a cone from left to right and eat immediately.

hand-rolled sushi

scattered sushi

1 quantity still warm prepared sushi rice (page 244)

2 tablespoons toasted white, black or mixed sesame seeds

2 spring onions (scallions), sliced

60 g (2¼ oz) simmered shiitake mushrooms, finely chopped (page 136)

50 g (1¾ oz) bamboo shoots, finely chopped

60 g (2¼ oz) prepared kanpyo (gourd strip), finely chopped

35 g (¼ cup) finely chopped pickled ginger

1 tablespoon Japanese rice vinegar

4 thin crepe-like omelettes, cut into very thin strips (page 225)

12 sugar snap peas or snow peas (mangetout), trimmed, lightly blanched

100 g (3½ oz) sashimi-grade tuna or salmon, cut into short, thin strips

12 cooked king prawns (shrimp), peeled and deveined

2 toasted nori sheets, cut into thin strips

Serves 4–6 as a main or 8 as a starter

Combine the sushi rice with the sesame seeds, spring onion, shiitake, bamboo shoots, kanpyo and pickled ginger in a large bowl. Spread the mixture over the base of a large, wide shallow serving bowl or lacquerware tray with sides.

Fill a bowl with warm water and mix in the rice vinegar. Dampen your hands with the vinegared water to prevent the rice sticking to your hands. Smooth the rice mixture into the bowl, dampening your hands as needed.

Sprinkle the omelette strips evenly over the top, then arrange or scatter the peas, sashimi strips, prawns and nori evenly over the top of that and serve immediately. Use a wooden rice paddle or spoon to serve into small bowls.

**450 g (1 lb) finest sashimi-grade tuna
or salmon fillet**
daikon, peeled, very finely julienned

CONDIMENTS
Japanese soy sauce
wasabi paste
finely grated fresh ginger
pickled ginger

Serves 4

Trim any skin, bloodline or dark flesh from the tuna. Slice into 2.5 cm (1 in) thick cutlets, then lay each cutlet down on a board and thinly slice along the width. Lay the pieces of tuna out and neaten the edges to give rectangles 6 cm (2½ in) wide. You should get at least 30 slices.

Divide the sashimi slices onto four individual platters in an overlapping row. Add a mound of finely julienned daikon and serve with soy sauce, wasabi paste and ginger on the side. Guests should use chopsticks to mix a little wasabi paste or fresh ginger into the soy sauce or simply smear a little of the wasabi paste onto the fish itself and dip into the soy sauce—it should not be dunked, as the strong flavour of the soy sauce will overpower the delicate flavour of the raw fish. Pickled ginger will refresh the palate.

sashimi

seaweed

The Japanese make the world's greatest use of *kaiso*, seaweed, and have been gathering hundreds of kinds from their coastal waters since prehistoric times. Seaweed harvest is even depicted in the eighth-century poetry anthology, *Manyoshu*, as well as in the woodblock prints of the Edo period (AD 1600–1868).

In seaside villages all around the country, there is evidence of the various seaweeds plucked from the depths and shallows by the villagers. There might be long strands of *konbu* hung over lines or stretched over the concrete at the edge of a parking lot, *nori* spread in sheets on small bamboo mats, or *tengusa* scattered on tarpaulins along the beach, all drying in the sun and intended for

household use. These fruits of the sea are also harvested, as well as cultivated, on a huge commercial scale.

Konbu, or kelp, is an essential ingredient in dashi, the stock that is used in so many ways in Japanese cooking. It can also be used as a wrapper around fillings, or can even be pickled. Wakame is added to salads and floated in soups. Nori sheets wrap sembei crackers, maki-zushi and o-nigiri, while flakes and slivers of it flavour and garnish many dishes. Seaweed is offered to the gods on shrine altars, and its renowned health-giving properties are said to contribute to the long lives of the Japanese people.

sake-glazed salmon

4 x 175 g (6 oz) salmon fillets
1 tablespoon vegetable oil
1 teaspoon sesame oil
40 g (1½ oz) unsalted butter
60 ml (¼ cup) sake
1½ tablespoons Japanese soy sauce
1 tablespoon mirin
2 teaspoons caster (superfine) sugar
¼ teaspoon finely grated fresh ginger

Serves 4 as a main

Check the salmon carefully for bones, pulling any you find out with clean tweezers. Season lightly with salt.

Heat the oils in a large heavy-based frying pan over medium–high heat. Add the salmon pieces, skin-side down, and cook for 3 minutes, or until the skin is golden. Reduce the heat to medium, turn the fish over and cook for a further 2–3 minutes, or until almost cooked through. Remove the salmon from the pan, cover and set aside.

Remove any excess oil from the pan then add the butter, sake, soy sauce, mirin, sugar and ginger to the pan. Increase the heat to high and stir to dissolve the sugar. Allow to come to the boil and cook, stirring, for 2 minutes, or until slightly thickened. Drizzle over the salmon. Great served with rice and steamed green vegetables.

8 raw king prawns (shrimp)
200 g (7 oz) piece of squid, opened out flat
200 g (7 oz) white fish fillet, cut into
  4 even pieces
½ small onion, cut into four thin wedges,
  with a toothpick securing each wedge
4 fresh shiitake mushrooms, stems discarded
4 very thin slices of jap pumpkin, unpeeled
1 baby eggplant (aubergine), cut into
  5 mm (¼ in) thick slices on the diagonal
½ small green capsicum (pepper), cut
  lengthways into quarters
4 shiso leaves, optional
4 nori strips, 8 x 3 cm (3 x 1¼ in),
  optional

plain (all-purpose) flour, for coating
2 quantities tempura batter, each quantity
  made just before you need it (page 247)
vegetable oil, for deep-frying
60 ml (¼ cup) sesame oil

CONDIMENTS
1 quantity tempura dipping sauce
  (page 247)
70 g (2½ oz) daikon, peeled, finely grated,
  then squeezed to remove excess liquid
2 teaspoons finely grated fresh ginger

Serves 4 as a main

Peel and devein the prawns, leaving the tails intact. Make three cuts in the belly of the prawns. Turn the prawns over and, starting from the tail end, press down gently at intervals along the length of the prawn—this helps to break the connective tissue, preventing the prawns from curling up too much. Finely score the squid in a crisscross pattern on both sides, then cut into 4 x 3 cm (1½ x 1¼ in) pieces. Arrange the seafood and vegetables on separate platters, cover with plastic wrap and refrigerate until ready to use.

Fill a deep-fat fryer or large saucepan one-third full of vegetable oil, then add the sesame oil. Heat to 180°C (350°F), or until a cube of bread dropped into the oil browns in 15 seconds. Dip each ingredient except the shiso and nori into the flour before battering.

Make one batch of batter. Starting with the onion and pumpkin, quickly dip into the batter, allowing the excess to drip off, then lower into the oil. Cook for 2–3 minutes, or until cooked through and the batter is lightly golden and crispy. It should also look lacy and a little see-through—if the batter is too thick, add a little more iced water. Drain on paper towels, then keep warm in a low oven while you cook the rest of the vegetables. Skim off any bits of floating batter as you cook. Make the second batch of batter and cook the seafood in small batches for 1–3 minutes, or until just cooked through and lightly golden and crispy. Keep warm in the oven. Serve with a small bowl of the dipping sauce with grated daikon and ginger mixed in according to taste.

tempura

seafood and vegetable fritters

300 g (10½ oz) raw prawns (shrimp),
  peeled and deveined
100 g (3½ oz) scallops, roe removed
1 small carrot, peeled
5 cm (2 in) piece of daikon
  (about 70 g/2½ oz), peeled
1 small onion
6 green beans
25 g (1 oz) mitsuba or flat-leaf (Italian)
  parsley with stems

1½ tablespoons plain (all-purpose) flour
vegetable oil, for deep-frying
60 ml (¼ cup) sesame oil
1 quantity tempura batter (page 247)
1 quantity tempura dipping sauce
  (page 247)

Serves 6–8 as a starter

Chop the prawns and scallops into small pieces. Cut the carrot and daikon into 4 cm (1½ in) lengths, then finely julienne, using a very sharp knife or Japanese mandolin with a medium-tooth blade. Cut the onion in half and finely slice. Finely slice the beans on the diagonal.

Cut the leaves from the mitsuba stems, then cut the stems into 4 cm (1½ in) lengths. Roughly chop the leaves.

Put the chopped seafood, julienned vegetables and mitsuba in a bowl with the flour and mix to combine.

Fill a deep-fat fryer or large saucepan one-third full of vegetable oil, then add the sesame oil. Heat to 170°C (325°F), or until a cube of bread dropped into the oil browns in 20 seconds.

Make the tempura batter. Lightly mix the seafood mixture through the tempura batter. Working in batches, drop heaped tablespoons of the mixture into the hot oil and cook for 3–4 minutes, or until crisp, golden and cooked through. Drain on paper towels and serve immediately with the dipping sauce.

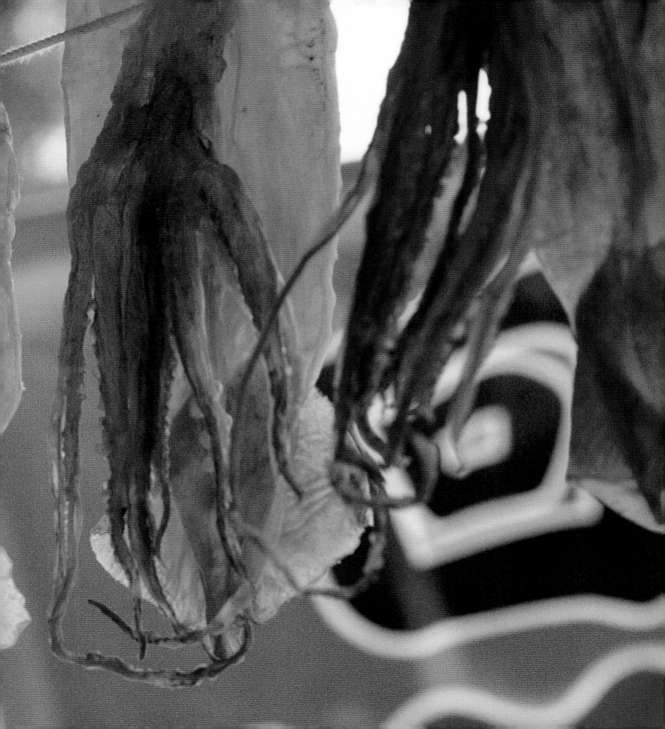

250 ml (1 cup) dashi II (page 245)
125 ml (½ cup) sake
80 ml (⅓ cup) mirin
60 ml (¼ cup) Japanese soy sauce
5 cm (2 in) piece of fresh ginger, peeled,
   thickly sliced
½ teaspoon black or dark brown sugar
2 whole cleaned baby snapper
   or other firm, white fish
   (about 450 g/1 lb each)
1 spring onion (scallion), thinly sliced
2 tablespoons finely grated daikon,
   squeezed to remove excess liquid

Serves 4 as a main

Combine the dashi, sake, mirin, soy sauce, ginger and sugar in a large, deep frying pan. Sit the pan over high heat and stir until the sugar has dissolved. Bring to the boil.

Using a sharp knife, slash the fish a couple of times on each side through the thickest part. Add the fish to the pan and allow the liquid to return to the boil, then immediately reduce to a simmer and cook for 5–7 minutes, or until the fish is opaque and just cooked through.

If you wish to serve the fish whole, do not turn it during cooking. Instead, continuously spoon the simmering liquid over the top of the fish to help promote more even cooking but note that the bottom side may be more cooked than the top. If you are less concerned with appearance and prefer a more even texture to the flesh, you can carefully turn the fish over halfway through cooking but note that the fish may break up a little.

Transfer the fish, keeping the top-side up, to a serving platter with a lip and spoon a little sauce over the top. Sprinkle with spring onion and serve immediately. Pass around a small dish of grated daikon to add to the fish. Accompany with rice and vegetable or salad sides.

whole fish
simmered in broth

salmon and miso hotpot

400 g (14 oz) daikon, peeled
2 litres (8 cups) dashi II (page 245)
100 g (⅓ cup) red miso
80 ml (⅓ cup) sake
60 ml (¼ cup) mirin
1 tablespoon Japanese soy sauce
8 small new potatoes, peeled
4 baby leeks, white part only, cut into
   5 cm (2 in) pieces
250 g (9 oz) Chinese cabbage, chopped
   into 5 cm (2 in) pieces

750 g (1 lb 10 oz) salmon fillet, cut
   into 5 cm (2 in) pieces
150 g (5½ oz) shimeji mushrooms,
   pulled apart
600 g (1 lb 5 oz) block silken firm tofu,
   cut into eight cubes
1 tablespoon red miso, extra
40 g (1½ oz) butter
ichimi togarashi (chilli powder) or shichimi
   togarashi (seven spice mix), optional

Serves 6 as a main

Cut the daikon into 3 cm (1¼ in) slices. Bevel the edges by running a sharp knife or vegetable peeler along the sharp edges so the shape is softened and slightly rounded.

Combine the dashi, miso, sake, mirin and soy sauce in a large flameproof casserole dish or Japanese *nabe* (cooking pot) and bring to the boil over high heat. Add the daikon and potatoes, bring back to the boil and cook for 18 minutes, or until the potatoes are just tender. Reduce to a simmer, add the leek and cabbage and, when the liquid starts to simmer again, cook for 3 minutes.

Add the salmon pieces and the shimeji and cook for 5 minutes, then make room for the tofu and cook for a few more minutes, or until the salmon is cooked through and the tofu is heated.

Remove the dish from the heat, stir in the extra miso, then add the butter and allow it to melt before gently stirring through, being careful not to break up the fish. Serve the hotpot at the table for guests to serve themselves. This is quite a substantial meal, but if you like you can add some hot cooked rice to the broth left at the end to make a soup to enjoy as the last course. Serve with the ichimi togarashi for sprinkling, if desired.

1 chicken thigh fillet
200 g (7 oz) white fish fillet
8 raw king prawns (shrimp)
8 scallops, beard and roe removed
8 oysters
1 carrot, peeled, very thinly sliced on the
    diagonal and blanched
2 baby leeks (white part only), cut into
    1 cm (½ in) pieces on the diagonal
8 fresh shiitake mushrooms
¼ Chinese cabbage, cut into 2 cm (¾ in)
    wide sections (keep the layers together)
8 spring onions (scallions), cut into 5 cm
    (2 in) lengths
150 g (5½ oz) snow peas (mangetout),
    trimmed
300 g (10½ oz) silken firm tofu, cut into
    eight pieces

60 g (2¼ oz) kamaboko (fish-paste loaf),
    sliced into 5 mm (¼ in) thick slices
50 g (1¾ oz) harusame (bean thread
    noodles), soaked in hot water for
    10 minutes
15 g (½ oz) mitsuba, flat-leaf (Italian)
    parsley or mizuna
1 quantity ponzu (page 246) or
    250 ml (1 cup) ready-made ponzu

BROTH
1.5 litres (6 cups) dashi II (page 245)
60 ml (¼ cup) Japanese soy sauce
2 tablespoons mirin
2 tablespoons sake

Serves 4 as a main

Cut the chicken and fish into 3 cm (1¼ in) pieces. Peel and devein the prawns, leaving the tails intact. Remove the vein, membrane or hard white muscle from the scallops. Loosen the oysters from their shells but leave in the shell. Arrange all the seafood, vegetables, tofu, kamaboko, noodles and mitsuba on a platter. Give each guest a small bowl of ponzu and a bowl of rice.

To make the broth, combine all the ingredients in a flameproof casserole dish over high heat. Bring to the boil, then reduce to a simmer.

Put the carrot and leeks in the broth first and cook for a few minutes, then add the shiitake, cabbage and chicken and cook for 2 minutes more. Add the fish and cook a further minute. One by one, add these ingredients to the pot in the following order: spring onion, snow peas, tofu, kamaboko, prawns, scallops, noodles and oysters—try to keep the ingredients grouped. Cook for 2–3 minutes, or until the seafood is just cooked through. Add the mitsuba at the end of cooking. Lift the pot onto the table and let everyone serve themselves from the pot. Dip each piece of food into the ponzu before eating.

Alternatively, heat the broth in a *nabe* (cooking pot) on a gas burner in the centre of the table. Each diner cooks their own ingredients in the broth.

mixed **hotpot**

a little taste of...

The seasons have great meaning for the Japanese and strongly influence their cuisine. Even with greenhouse cultivation and aquaculture now assuring that many vegetables are available year-round, certain ones remain meaningful symbols of various times of the year, and people find particular pleasure in anticipating and relishing their arrival. Every shopping street has a convenient open-front vegetable shop or two, with their crates of goods stacked out to the edge of the pavement. Shops and supermarkets sell not only *yasai*, cultivated vegetables, but also proffer a variety of wild plants called *sansai*—mountain vegetables such as fern fiddleheads and butterbur buds. Farmers' markets, *ichiba*, are a rarity in Japan these days. However, in some rural or semi-rural areas, elderly country women still tie baskets of garden produce to their backs and catch the train to a major station where they squat along walkways and peddle their goods to passersby. The Japanese obsession with perfection in food has an impact on the produce offered for sale—fruit or vegetables with even the most minor imperfection will be left in the field to be ploughed under as fertilizer.

...vegetable market

spinach with sesame dressing

1 large bunch (about 200 g/7 oz) English
   spinach, stems trimmed
Japanese soy sauce, for sprinkling

DRESSING
50 g (⅓ cup) white or black sesame seeds
1½ teaspoons caster (superfine) sugar
1 tablespoon sake
1½ tablespoons dashi II (page 245)
2 teaspoons tamari

Serves 4–6 as a side

Rinse the spinach thoroughly to remove any grit. Bring a saucepan of salted water to the boil, add the spinach and cook for 1 minute. Drain and plunge into iced water to stop the cooking process, then drain well again. Wrap in a tea towel or bamboo sushi mat and squeeze out any excess moisture. Sprinkle lightly with a little soy sauce, allow to cool, then cut into 3 cm (1¼ in) lengths.

To make the dressing, dry-fry the sesame seeds over medium heat, stirring regularly, for about 5 minutes, or until lightly golden and aromatic. Immediately scoop into a *suribachi* (ribbed mortar) or normal mortar, reserving 1 teaspoon of whole seeds for garnish, if desired, and grind until very finely crushed. Gradually incorporate the sugar, sake, dashi and tamari until it forms a smooth paste.

Just before serving, toss the spinach and dressing together and transfer to the centre of a small serving dish. Sprinkle with the reserved toasted sesame seeds, if using.

**200 g (7 oz) daikon (about one-third
   of a daikon)**
1 carrot
80 ml (⅓ cup) Japanese rice vinegar
2 tablespoons caster (superfine) sugar
**4 cm (1½ in) square piece of konbu, wiped
   with a damp cloth and cut into
   1 cm (½ in) wide strips**
1 teaspoon black sesame seeds, optional

Serves 6–8 as a side

Peel the daikon and carrot, then cut into 5 cm (2 in) lengths. Very finely
julienne both, either by using a Japanese mandolin with the medium-tooth
blade or by very thinly slicing the 5 cm (2 in) pieces and then cutting these
slices into very thin strips. Put the julienned vegetables in a colander and
sprinkle with salt. Stand for 30 minutes, then rinse and drain well, squeezing
out any excess moisture.

Meanwhile, to make the dressing combine the rice vinegar with the sugar
and ¼ teaspoon salt and stir until the sugar and salt have dissolved.

Transfer the daikon and carrot mixture to a non-metallic bowl, add the
konbu, then pour over the dressing and stir together. Cover with plastic wrap
and refrigerate for 24–48 hours, stirring occasionally. When ready to serve,
remove the konbu and discard. Drain the vegetables well, discarding the
liquid. Scoop into a serving dish and, if you like, sprinkle with black sesame
seeds. Serve. This is an especially good accompaniment to fried foods.

daikon and carrot salad

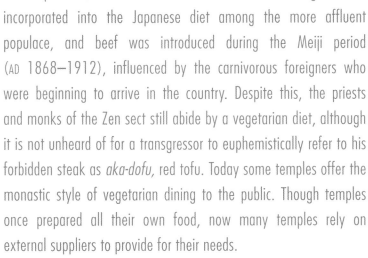

vegetarian food... The imaginative use of a vast array of vegetables, both wild and cultivated, has a long history in Japan. Buddhism's proscription against killing any living creature meant that as the religion spread throughout Japan over 1,000 years ago, so too did vegetarian food.

It was in the Buddhist Zen temples that vegetarian cooking developed into a sophisticated art. Known as *shojin ryori,* this way of eating is one of the essential ascetic practices for the monks in their progress toward enlightenment. In the Zen kitchen, food is considered a sort of medicine for the body, but one that should also bring enjoyment. Each ingredient should be fresh, prepared in a suitable manner and without any waste. Before eating, it is customary for monks to recite Zen's grace, a series of reflections that nurture in them a sense of gratitude.

During the Edo period (AD 1600–1868) chicken and rabbit began to be incorporated into the Japanese diet among the more affluent populace, and beef was introduced during the Meiji period (AD 1868–1912), influenced by the carnivorous foreigners who were beginning to arrive in the country. Despite this, the priests and monks of the Zen sect still abide by a vegetarian diet, although it is not unheard of for a transgressor to euphemistically refer to his forbidden steak as *aka-dofu,* red tofu. Today some temples offer the monastic style of vegetarian dining to the public. Though temples once prepared all their own food, now many temples rely on external suppliers to provide for their needs.

Although true vegetarianism is quite rare in Japan today, vegetables predominate in traditional cuisine, for the Japanese love their great variety as well as their unique ways of preparation.

grilled eggplant
with dashi

6 baby or slender eggplants (aubergines)
vegetable oil, for brushing
60 ml (¼ cup) dashi II (page 245)
1½ tablespoons Japanese soy sauce
1 teaspoon mirin
½ teaspoon grated fresh ginger
    with its juice
pinch of caster (superfine) sugar
fine katsuobushi (bonito flakes), to
    garnish, optional

Serves 6–8 as a side

Preheat a griller (broiler) to high. Brush the eggplants with oil, then prick a few times with a skewer. Put the eggplants under the griller and cook for 12–15 minutes, turning regularly until the skin is slightly blackened and wrinkled and the flesh feels soft to the touch. Immediately plunge into iced water until cool enough to handle, then peel, discarding the skin. Cut the flesh into 5 cm (2 in) lengths. Place in an attractive bundle in a serving dish.

Combine the dashi, soy sauce, mirin, ginger and juice, and sugar and pour over the eggplant. If you are using the katsuobushi, sprinkle it over the top of the dish just before serving.

700 g (1 lb 9 oz) jap or butternut pumpkin
   (squash), unpeeled
185 ml (¾ cup) dashi II (page 245)
2 tablespoons mirin
1½ tablespoons Japanese soy sauce
3 teaspoons caster (superfine) sugar
sesame seeds, toasted, for garnish

Serves 6–8 as a side

Cut the pumpkin into rough 4 cm (1½ in) cubes. Peel just around the edges
of the skin on each piece, then bevel the edges by running a sharp knife or
vegetable peeler along the sharp edges so the cube shape is softened and
slightly rounded.

Put the pumpkin in a saucepan and cover with cold water. Bring to the boil
over high heat and cook for about 5 minutes, or until it just begins to become
tender. Drain well.

Combine the dashi, mirin, soy sauce, sugar and ½ teaspoon salt in a clean
saucepan over high heat, stirring until the sugar has dissolved. Add the
pumpkin skin-side down and bring the liquid to the boil. Reduce to a simmer,
then continue cooking for about 15 minutes, or until the liquid has almost all
been absorbed by the pumpkin. Do not stir but carefully turn once halfway
through cooking.

Carefully pile the pumpkin into a serving bowl, drizzle with any remaining
sauce and sprinkle with toasted sesame seeds.

sweet simmered pumpkin

mushrooms with ponzu dressing

200 g (7 oz) fresh shiitake mushrooms
1 tablespoon vegetable oil
60 ml (¼ cup) ponzu (page 246) or
 ready-made ponzu
sesame oil, for drizzling, optional

Serves 4–6 as a side

Remove the stems from the shiitake and discard. Cut any larger caps in half.

Heat the oil in a frying pan over medium–high heat, add the shiitake and season with salt. Cook on each side for 2 minutes, or until tender.

Transfer to a shallow bowl and immediately pour over the ponzu and, if you like, drizzle with a little sesame oil.

DRESSING
200 g (7 oz) silken firm tofu
50 g (⅓ cup) sesame seeds, toasted
1 tablespoon caster (superfine) sugar
1 tablespoon white miso
1 tablespoon dashi II (page 245)
2 teaspoons Japanese soy sauce
3 teaspoons mirin
3 teaspoons sake

SALAD
100 g (3½ oz) konnyaku (yam cake)
1 small carrot
170 ml (⅔ cup) dashi II (page 245)
1 tablespoon mirin
3 teaspoons Japanese soy sauce
12 baby green beans, cut into 3 cm (1¼ in) lengths
6 fresh shiitake mushrooms, stems discarded, caps sliced

Serves 6–8 as a side

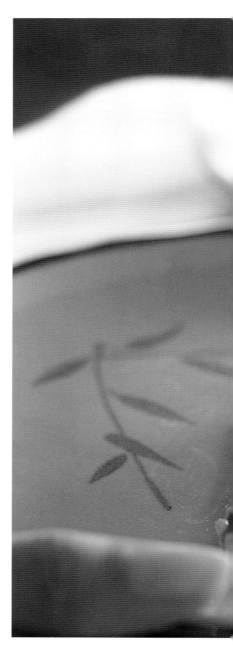

To **weight** the tofu, wrap it in a clean tea towel. Put two plates on top of the tofu and leave for about 2 hours to extract any excess moisture.

Meanwhile, start preparing the salad. Boil the konnyaku for 2 minutes, then cut into 3 cm x 5 mm (1¼ x ¼ in) strips. Peel the carrot, then cut at 5 cm (2 in) intervals along the carrot so you have three or four chunks. Now slice each chunk lengthways into 5 mm (¼ in) wide strips. Lay each strip on its side and cut into1 cm (½ in) wide strips along its length.

Combine the dashi, mirin and soy sauce in a saucepan and bring to the boil over high heat. Reduce to a simmer, then add the carrot, konnyaku and beans and cook for 3 minutes, or until the carrot is tender. Remove the vegetables with a slotted spoon and set aside. Add the shiitake to the pan, increase the heat to high and cook for 1–2 minutes, or until the liquid has almost evaporated. Cool completely.

Remove the tofu from the tea towel, then pat dry with paper towels. Finely mash the tofu with the back of a fork and set aside.

To **make** the dressing, grind the sesame seeds in a *suribachi* (ribbed mortar) or mortar and pestle until finely crushed, then gradually mix in the sugar, miso, dashi, soy sauce, mirin and sake until smooth. Stir the tofu into the mixture.

Put the cooled carrot and shiitake mixtures in a bowl with the dressing and toss to combine. Serve in a neat mound in one large serving bowl or in small individual dishes.

white salad

sautéed burdock

250 g (9 oz) gobo (burdock root)
2 teaspoons Japanese rice vinegar
1 small carrot, peeled
1½ tablespoons vegetable oil
1 teaspoon sesame oil
1½ tablespoons sake
1½ tablespoons mirin
2 teaspoons caster (superfine) sugar
2½ tablespoons Japanese soy sauce
shichimi togarashi (seven spice mix), for
    sprinkling, optional

Serves 6–8 as a side or snack

Roughly scrape the skin of the gobo with a sharp knife, then cut into 5 cm (2 in) pieces and finely julienne. Put the julienned strips into a bowl with 625 ml (2½ cups) water and the rice vinegar. Leave for about 15 minutes to remove some of the bitterness from the gobo. Drain well.

Meanwhile, cut the carrot into 5 cm (2 in) lengths, then finely julienne.

Heat the vegetable and sesame oils in a saucepan over medium–high heat, then add the gobo and carrot and stir to combine well with the oil. Cook for about 10 minutes, or until lightly golden and softened.

Add the sake, mirin, sugar and 1 tablespoon water to the pan and cook, stirring regularly, for about 5 minutes, or until the liquid is almost absorbed, then add the soy sauce and cook for a further 2 minutes. Remove from the heat and serve hot or spread out on a plate and allow to cool—the flavour will improve on sitting for a few hours. Divide among small dishes and, if you like, sprinkle with shichimi togarashi before serving.

**2 bunches (300 g/10½ oz) of asparagus,
trimmed and cut in half**

SAUCE
3 egg yolks
60 ml (¼ cup) Japanese rice vinegar
1 tablespoon mirin
2 teaspoons caster (superfine) sugar
2 tablespoons dashi I (page 245)

Serves 4–6 as a side

Bring a saucepan of lightly salted water to the boil. Add the asparagus and cook for 1 minute, or until just tender. Drain and plunge into iced water to stop the cooking process. Drain well.

To make the sauce, put all the ingredients in a small saucepan and whisk to combine well. Sit the pan over low heat and stir the sauce constantly for 3–4 minutes, or until smooth and thickened slightly. Remove from the heat. Put the pan on top of a bowl of ice and stir until cold.

Arrange the asparagus on a serving plate with the tips all facing one direction, then pour over the sauce, avoiding the tips.

asparagus with egg yolk sauce

pickles

In Japan, as in the West, pickles provide crunch, colour and flavourful contrast to main meals. The difference is that the Japanese regard pickles as absolutely essential to the meal, so they even appear on the breakfast table.

These *tsukemono* exist in incredible variety. Among the most popular are the daikon radish, daikon greens, Chinese cabbage, cucumber, eggplant (aubergine) and ginger, but almost any vegetable can be, and is, pickled. Only sometimes vinegared, these 'pickled things' are more often preserved and thereby flavoured with *nuka* (rice bran), salt or *miso*. There is a particular freshness to many Japanese pickles, for they are typically processed for only a brief period of time and intended to be consumed relatively soon.

Every region of the country has its own pickle specialities and they are even sold around famous tourist destinations as souvenirs to take home for friends and relatives. The venerable 'Kintame' in Kyoto is one such shop where visitors can not only supply themselves with packets of quite wondrous pickles, but also book a table for a simple but splendid lunch of rice, soup and what is, in fact, the main course: a colourful and delectable palette of assorted *tsukemono*. Pickles are the perfect accompaniment to rice and in less affluent times in Japan they were often the only one.

しその実　きゃらふき　実とうがらし　なめ味噌　金山寺味噌　わさび漬　からし漬　与一漬

名産
うりのてっぽう漬

simmered daikon

1 small daikon (about 600 g/1 lb 5 oz)
625 ml (2½ cups) dashi II (page 245)
2 tablespoons Japanese soy sauce
1 tablespoon mirin
2 teaspoons sugar
5 cm (2 in) square piece of konbu, wiped
   with a damp cloth

Serves 4–6 as a side

Peel the daikon and cut into 3 cm (1¼ in) thick slices. Bevel the edges by running a sharp knife or vegetable peeler along the sharp edges so the shape is softened and slightly rounded—this helps the daikon to retain its shape when cooking. Cut a shallow cross on one of the flat sides of the daikon.

Put the daikon, cross-side down, in a large saucepan. Cover generously with water and bring to the boil, then reduce to a simmer and cook for 45 minutes, or until translucent. Drain.

Combine the dashi, soy sauce, mirin, sugar and konbu in a clean saucepan and bring to the boil, stirring until the sugar has dissolved. Add the daikon and allow to just come to the boil again. Reduce to a simmer, cover and cook for 30 minutes, or until soft but not breaking up.

To serve, put the konbu in the base of a shallow bowl, then stack the daikon on top and ladle over a little sauce.

**250 g (9 oz) green beans, trimmed and
cut into 5 cm (2 in) lengths**

DRESSING
50 g (⅓ cup) sesame seeds
1 teaspoon sugar
2 tablespoons red or white miso
2 tablespoons mirin

Serves 4–6 as a side

Bring a saucepan of lightly salted water to the boil. Add the beans and cook
for 2 minutes, or until just tender. Drain, plunge into iced water until cool,
then drain well.

To make the dressing, dry-fry the sesame seeds over medium heat, stirring
regularly, for about 5 minutes, or until lightly golden and aromatic. Immediately
scoop into a *suribachi* (ribbed mortar) or normal mortar, reserving 1 teaspoon
of whole seeds for garnish, if you like, and grind until very finely crushed.
Gradually incorporate the sugar, miso and mirin until it forms a thickish paste.

Put the beans in a bowl with the dressing and toss to combine. Serve in a
mound in a bowl or on a plate. Sprinkle with the reserved sesame seeds, if using.

beans with
sesame miso dressing

pumpkin with
pickled plum dressing

DRESSING
40 g (1½ oz) umeboshi (pickled plums)
   (about 5 small) or 1½–2 tablespoons
   pickled plum purée
2 teaspoons Japanese soy sauce
1 tablespoon mirin
2 tablespoons dashi II (page 245)
¼ teaspoon caster (superfine) sugar

500 g (1 lb 2 oz) jap pumpkin, unpeeled
   and seeded
2 teaspoons very finely shredded shiso
   leaves or 1 thinly sliced spring onion
   (scallion)

Serves 6–8 as a side

To make the dressing, if you are using pickled plums, prick them all over with a fork, then soak in cold water for 2 hours, changing the water occasionally— this helps remove the excess salt. Drain and pat dry, then remove the seeds and purée the flesh in a food processor or push through a fine sieve. Put the puréed plums or ready-made purée in a small bowl with the remaining dressing ingredients and stir to combine well.

Cut the pumpkin into 4 cm (1½ in) cubes. Peel just around the edges of the skin on each piece, then bevel the edges by running a sharp knife or vegetable peeler along the sharp edges so the cube shape is softened and slightly rounded.

Bring a saucepan of lightly salted water to the boil, then add the pumpkin and cook for 10–12 minutes, or until tender but not mushy. Drain well and set aside to cool to room temperature.

Lightly toss the cooled pumpkin with the dressing, then pile neatly into a serving dish. Sprinkle with the finely sliced shiso leaves or spring onion.

o-bento

The Japanese box lunch is an art form in itself. The simplest consists of nothing more than a red pickled plum called *umeboshi* centred on a square field of white rice, looking just like the Japanese flag. This *hinomaru bento* is a bittersweet reminder of past times when poverty allowed no more than an extremely modest, yet tasty, meal such as this.

The good Japanese wife and mother, even now that many women are employed outside the home, gets up early so she can prepare nutritious, delicious boxed lunches for her family, filled with many small morsels of various

flavours, colours and textures. Children and husbands alike take pleasure and quiet pride in this typically unspoken expression of love.

Outside the home, *bento* boxes are sold in their millions every day. Supermarkets and convenience stores provide big *bento* selections to suit nearly every taste. One of the special delights of long-distance train travel is the *ekiben*, station lunch. Whether bought from a cart passing up the aisle or from a platform vendor, it offers specialities of its particular region. There are also special 'between act' *bento* for theatre patrons, and *kaiseki bento* for guests at a tea ceremony.

8 large dried shiitake mushrooms
375 ml (1½ cups) dashi II (page 245) or
　konbu dashi II (page 246)
2 tablespoons mirin
2 tablespoons sake
2 tablespoons Japanese soy sauce
1 tablespoon dark brown sugar

Serves 4–6 as a side

Soak the shiitake in hot water for 30 minutes, then drain well. Discard the stems.

Combine the dashi, mirin, sake, soy sauce and sugar in a small saucepan, sit the pan over high heat and stir until the sugar has dissolved. Bring to the boil. Add the shiitake, return to the boil, then reduce to a simmer and cook for 1 hour, or until the liquid has almost evaporated.

Serve warm or at room temperature in a small bowl as a condiment, part of a multicourse meal or served over rice as a snack. Simmered shiitake can also be thinly sliced to use in sushi or savoury Japanese custard.

shiitake
simmered in soy

corn with soy

2 corn cobs, cut into thirds
25 g (1 oz) butter, melted
2 teaspoons Japanese soy sauce
1½ teaspoons mirin
1 teaspoon caster (superfine) sugar

Serves 6 as a side or 2 as a snack

Bring a saucepan of water to the boil over high heat, then add the corn. Cook for 3 minutes, then drain well.

Preheat the griller (broiler) to high.

Combine the butter, soy sauce, mirin and sugar, then brush the mixture over the corn on a foil-lined tray and place under the hot griller. Cook for 2–3 minutes, turning and basting regularly until golden and slightly blistered.

vegetable oil, for cooking
1 teaspoon sesame oil
1 onion, cut into thin wedges
1 carrot, peeled, thinly sliced on the
  diagonal
1 teaspoon grated fresh ginger
6 fresh shiitake mushrooms, stems
  discarded, caps sliced
½ green capsicum (pepper), thinly sliced
90 g (2 cups) sliced Chinese cabbage
90 g (1 cup) bean sprouts
1 tablespoon Japanese soy sauce or tamari
1 tablespoon mirin
pinch of ground white pepper
toasted sesame seeds, to garnish, optional

Serves 4–6 as a side

Heat a little vegetable oil and the sesame oil in a wok or large frying pan over high heat, add the onion and stir-fry for 2 minutes, or until lightly golden.

Add the carrot and stir-fry for another minute. Add the ginger, shiitake, capsicum and cabbage and stir-fry for 2 minutes, or until the cabbage has wilted slightly. Add the bean sprouts, soy sauce, mirin and a pinch of white pepper and stir-fry for another minute. Serve immediately, garnished with toasted sesame seeds, if you wish.

vegetable stir-fry

a little taste of...

Although gourmet Japanese cuisine can sometimes seem almost ethereal, home cooking is quite down to earth. There are many Japanese families who only rarely dine on sophisticated, multi-course fare, perhaps only on very special occasions. Instead they rely on simple and wholesome home-style meals that can be easily prepared in a short period of time, in typically limited kitchen space, while keeping within the household budget. *Ichiju issai* describes a basic meal pattern of one soup plus one fish or meat dish with a vegetable side. Of course, a bowl or two of rice is essential, and pickles may also be present on the table, but these are so ubiquitous that they do not even need to be mentioned. One-pot meals are extremely popular at home, such as the meat or fish and vegetable hotpot, *nabemono,* which is prepared at the table over a portable gas ring. Another favourite one-pot meal is *donburi,* which consists of bowls of rice with various savoury meat and vegetable toppings. Even *sushi* might be prepared at home, but not the skill-intensive version of the *sushiya* master, rather a simpler form such as *inarizushi.*

...home-style cooking

miso soup

1½ teaspoons dried wakame pieces
200 g (7 oz) silken firm tofu, cut into
   1.5 cm (⅝ in) cubes
1 spring onion (scallion), thinly sliced
875 ml (3½ cups) dashi II (page 245) or
   konbu dashi II (page 246)
100 g (⅓ cup) red or white miso, or a
   mixture of both

Serves 4 as a starter

Soak the wakame in cold water for 5 minutes, or until rehydrated and glossy but not mushy. Drain well, then divide among four small Japanese soup bowls or Chinese rice bowls. Divide the tofu and the spring onion among the bowls.

Pour the dashi into a saucepan and bring to the boil.

Combine the miso with 250 ml (1 cup) of the dashi stock in a bowl. Whisk until smooth. Return the miso mixture to the saucepan and stir until combined—be careful not to boil the broth as this will diminish the flavour of the miso. Ladle into the bowls until they are two-thirds full. Serve immediately.

Sip the miso soup from the bowl—rest the bowl in your left hand and tilt to your lips with your right. You can use chopsticks to eat the solid ingredients.

100 g (3½ oz) konnyaku (yam cake), cut
  into 1.5 cm (⅝ in) dice, optional
100 g (3½ oz) gobo (burdock root)
1 teaspoon Japanese rice vinegar
1 litre (4 cups) dashi II (page 245)
200 g (7 oz) pork belly, cut into small
  bite-sized pieces
4 large fresh shiitake mushrooms, sliced
100 g (3½ oz) daikon, peeled, cut into
  quarters lengthways, then thickly sliced

1 carrot, peeled, cut into quarters
  lengthways, then thickly sliced
2½ tablespoons red miso
150 g (5½ oz) silken firm tofu, cut into
  1.5 cm (⅝ in) dice
1 teaspoon ginger juice, optional
  (page 247)
1 spring onion (scallion), thinly sliced

Serves 4 as a starter

Bring a small saucepan of water to the boil, add the konnyaku and cook for
1 minute. Drain well.

Roughly scrape the skin of the gobo with a sharp knife, then rinse. Starting
at the thin end, shave thinly with a knife (as if you are sharpening a pencil),
turning the gobo as you cut. Put the shavings into a bowl with 500 ml
(2 cups) water and the rice vinegar. Leave for about 15 minutes to remove
some of the bitterness from the gobo. Drain well.

Pour the dashi into a large saucepan and bring to the boil. Add the pork,
shiitake, daikon, carrot, gobo and konnyaku and allow it to return to the boil.
Reduce to a simmer and cook for 1 hour, or until the pork is cooked through
and tender.

Add the miso and stir until dissolved. Gently stir in the tofu and, if you are
using it, the ginger juice and divide among four small soup bowls. Sprinkle
with the spring onion and serve immediately.

pork and vegetable soup

rice soup

165 g (¾ cup) Japanese short-grain rice
1 litre (4 cups) dashi II (page 245)
1½ tablespoons Japanese soy sauce
2 teaspoons mirin
2 teaspoons sake
200 g (7 oz) cooked chopped chicken or
    prawns (shrimp)
2 eggs, lightly beaten
1 teaspoon ginger juice (page 247)
2 spring onions (scallions), finely chopped

Serves 4–6 as a main

Rinse the rice in cold water three to four times until it runs clear. (Some Japanese rice has already been through this washing process—it will be labelled on the packet.)

Combine the rice and dashi in a large saucepan and bring to the boil. Cover and reduce the heat to very low. Cook for 1 hour, stirring occasionally so the rice doesn't catch on the base of the pan. In the last 10 minutes of cooking, add the soy sauce, mirin and sake and stir to combine. Add the chicken or prawns.

Just before serving, stir in the egg and ginger juice and cook for 1 minute, or until the egg just starts to set. Serve in deep soup bowls sprinkled with spring onion.

**20 pieces inari abura-age (prepared
     deep-fried tofu sheets)**
1 quantity prepared sushi rice (page 244)
20 chives, optional

CONDIMENTS
Japanese soy sauce
wasabi paste, optional
pickled ginger, optional

Makes 20 pieces

Put the prepared inari abura-age in a colander and drain off any excess
liquid. Carefully insert a finger into the slit side of the sheets and gently prise
the pocket open, trying not to split the sheets. Repeat with the remaining inari
abura-age.

Fill each pocket with approximately 2 tablespoons of sushi rice then fold over
the open ends to enclose the rice as much as possible. You can dress these up
by tying a chive around the middle and securing with a knot at the top—this
also helps hold the open ends together to prevent the rice from falling out. Put
the sushi rice pockets, seam-side down, on a platter.

Serve with a small bowl of soy sauce for dipping into, and, if desired, a little
wasabi paste on the side to mix into the sauce and some pickled ginger as
a palate refresher.

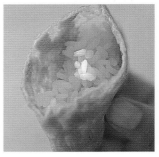

sushi rice in pockets

rice... Much of Japan's rural land is devoted to the cultivation of its staple crop. From late spring to autumn, it is a special pleasure to travel through rice country, as the burgeoning plants change from lush green to ripe gold. A particularly wonderful but rare sight is the terraces of *senmai-da,* the so-called 'thousand paddies', which were long ago carved out of otherwise unfarmable hillsides, and are now classified as protected cultural assets.

The significance of rice in Japan is immense. Cultivated for over 2,000 years, it has come to form the absolute foundation of the diet. Rice can also be said to have shaped Japanese society, for it was the cooperative effort required to

produce it successfully that nurtured the industriousness and group affinity for which the country is so well known.

Rice has long been considered sacred, a gift to the people from the gods, and Shinto observances accompany every important stage of the rice growing cycle. More than 40,000 Shinto shrines are dedicated to Inari-san, the deity of rice and commerce, and it is Inari's fox messenger which is famously and ubiquitously depicted at the shrines. The very popular deep-fried tofu skin pockets filled with vinegared rice are called *inarizushi* because they are said to be the favourite food of foxes.

The paramount position of rice can also be inferred from its special vocabulary. On the stalk it is known as *ine;* harvested but raw it is called *kome;* and cooked, *gohan*. Revealingly, *gohan* is also the word for meal. *Asa gohan* is breakfast, or 'morning rice'; *hiru gohan* is lunch, or 'noon rice'; and *ban gohan* is dinner, 'evening rice'.

Japonica rice, with its medium and somewhat glutinous grains and very subtle aroma, is the overwhelming preference of the Japanese. The grains of the cooked rice cling together, so it is suitable to eat using chopsticks. When a Japanese meal is arranged on the table, the rice bowl is positioned directly in front of the diner, with other dishes peripheral to it, for rice is the main dish and everything else mere accompaniment.

Rice consumption has been dwindling for several decades as a greater variety of foreign foods have become available. Yet most people still eat rice at least once and often twice a day and for many a meal is not fulfilling without a bowl of *gohan*. Life in industrial Japan does mean that for most Japanese, rice no longer comes directly from the field, but from a shop or even a vending machine.

five-flavoured rice

440 g (2 cups) Japanese short-grain rice
5 dried shiitake mushrooms
25 g (1 oz) abura-age (deep-fried tofu
   sheets)
100 g (3½ oz) konnyaku (yam cake),
   optional
1 small carrot, peeled
75 g (2½ oz) bamboo shoots
500 g (1 lb 2 oz) chicken thigh fillets,
   cut into bite-sized pieces

500 ml (2 cups) dashi II (page 245)
80 ml (⅓ cup) Japanese soy sauce
2 tablespoons mirin
7 g (¼ cup) chopped mitsuba or flat-leaf
   (Italian) parsley, optional

Serves 4–6 as a main

Rinse the rice several times in cold water until the water runs clear, then soak in fresh water for 1 hour.

Meanwhile, soak the shiitake in 375 ml (1½ cups) hot water for 30 minutes, then drain well, reserving the liquid. Discard the stems and thinly slice the caps.

Put the abura-age in a heatproof bowl and cover with boiling water for a few minutes. Drain and squeeze the sheets gently between paper towels to remove excess oil.

Cut the konnyaku, carrot, bamboo shoots and abura-age into 3 cm x 5 mm (1¼ x ¼ in) strips and put in a bowl with the mushrooms. Add the chicken pieces to the bowl.

Combine the dashi, reserved mushroom liquid, soy sauce, mirin and 1 teaspoon salt in a bowl, then pour over the chicken and vegetables and allow to sit for about 20 minutes.

Drain the rice and spread over the base of a large saucepan. Pour the chicken and vegetable mixture over but do not stir. Sit the saucepan over high heat and bring to the boil, then cover, reduce the heat to low and cook for 15 minutes. Turn off the heat, leaving the pan on the stove, and leave to stand for another 10 minutes before stirring to combine all the ingredients well. If you like, stir in the mitsuba, then serve.

275 g (1¼ cups) Japanese short-grain rice
2 eggs
2 tablespons dashi II (page 245) or
    instant dashi (page 246)
2 teaspoons sake
1 teaspoon sugar
pinch of ground white pepper
1 tablespoon Japanese soy sauce
vegetable oil, for pan-frying
2 teaspoons sesame oil
2 spring onions (scallions), chopped

4 fresh shiitake mushrooms, stems
    discarded, caps sliced
50 g (1¾ oz) bamboo shoots, thinly
    sliced
50 g (1¾ oz) sliced ham, cut into strips
40 g (¼ cup) frozen green peas, thawed
1 teaspoon finely chopped pickled ginger
1 spring onion (scallion), extra, sliced on
    the diagonal

Serves 4 as a main or 8 as a side

Rinse the rice several times in cold water until the water runs clear, then drain in a colander for 1 hour. Put in a saucepan with 375 ml (1½ cups) water. Bring to the boil, then cover with a tight-fitting lid, reduce the heat to low and simmer for 15 minutes. Turn off the heat but leave the pan on the hotplate. Working quickly, remove the lid, lay a clean tea towel over the top, then put the lid on and allow to sit for 15 minutes. Cool completely, then rinse well.

Put the eggs, dashi, sake, sugar, white pepper and 2 teaspoons of the soy sauce in a bowl and mix well. Heat a little of the vegetable oil in a small non-stick frying pan over medium heat, then add the egg mixture. Drag the egg mixture into the centre of the pan with a wooden spoon a couple of times and allow the mixture to flow back to the edges. Cook for 1 minute, or until almost set, then flip over and cook for a further 30 seconds. Remove and allow to cool. Roll the omelette up, then slice thinly.

Pour a little more vegetable oil and half the sesame oil into a wok or large frying pan and heat over medium heat. Add the spring onions, shiitake and bamboo shoots and stir-fry for 2 minutes, then add the ham and peas and stir-fry for a further 2 minutes. Remove from the wok.

Add a little more vegetable oil and the remaining sesame oil to the wok and add the rice. Stir-fry for 2 minutes, then return the mushroom mixture to the wok along with the remaining soy sauce and the pickled ginger and stir-fry to combine and heat through. Scoop into a bowl, then top with the egg and spring onion. Serve immediately.

japanese
fried rice

chicken and egg rice bowl

550 g (2½ cups) Japanese short-grain rice
375 ml (1½ cups) dashi II (page 245)
2 tablespoons sake
60 ml (¼ cup) mirin
80 ml (⅓ cup) Japanese soy sauce
500 g (1 lb 2 oz) chicken thigh fillets,
**   cut into bite-sized pieces**
1 onion, cut in half, then sliced into
**   wedges**

10–12 mitsuba leaves
4 spring onions (scallions), cut into 3 cm
**   (1¼ in) lengths**
6 eggs, stirred to lightly combine
nori flakes or strips, to garnish, optional
shichimi togarashi (seven spice mix),
**   optional**

Serves 4

Rinse the rice several times in cold water until the water runs clear, then drain in a colander for 1 hour. Put in a saucepan with 750 ml (3 cups) water. Bring to the boil, then cover with a tight-fitting lid, reduce the heat to low and simmer for 15 minutes. Turn off the heat but leave the pan on the hotplate. Working quickly, remove the lid, lay a clean tea towel over the top, then put the lid on and allow to stand for 15 minutes.

Combine the dashi, sake, mirin and soy sauce in a small saucepan and bring to the boil. Add the chicken and onion and return to the boil. Reduce to a simmer and cook for about 7 minutes, or until the chicken is tender. Skim off any scum that forms on the surface.

Scatter the mitsuba and spring onion over the top of the chicken mixture, then pour the egg over in a circular motion but do not stir—simply allow the egg to flow naturally over the other ingredients. Cook for 1 minute, or until the egg is just starting to set around the edges. Turn off the heat and cover. Rest for 2–3 minutes, or until the egg is half set.

Divide the hot rice among four wide, deep bowls, then evenly divide the chicken and egg mixture among the bowls. The heat of the rice will continue to cook the egg. If you like, sprinkle with nori and serve immediately. Pass the shichimi togarashi for those who wish to sprinkle it over the top.

SAUCE
375 ml (1½ cups) dashi II (page 245)
80 ml (⅓ cup) Japanese soy sauce
1 tablespoon mirin
2 g (⅓ cup) katsuobushi (bonito flakes)

15 cm (6 in) square piece of konbu, wiped
    with a damp cloth
600 g (1 lb 5 oz) block silken firm tofu,
    cut into six pieces

CONDIMENTS
finely grated fresh ginger
finely shredded nori
thinly sliced spring onions (scallions)
fine katsuobushi (bonito flakes)
toasted sesame seeds

Serves 6 as a light meal

To make the sauce, combine the dashi, soy sauce and mirin in a small saucepan and bring to the boil, then reduce to a simmer. Add the bonito flakes and remove from the heat. Allow the bonito to settle to the bottom, then strain the liquid into a smaller saucepan and keep warm over a low heat until ready to use. Pour into a vessel with a pouring lip for serving.

Pour 1.25 litres (5 cups) water into a *nabe* or flameproof casserole dish and add the konbu. Set aside to soak for 2 hours.

Sit the *nabe* over a portable gas burner or electric hotplate at the dinner table and bring to the boil over high heat. Reduce to a simmer and add the tofu. Return to a simmer and cook for 2–3 minutes, or until heated through. Turn off the heat. It is important to cook the tofu at a low heat to retain its silken texture—if cooked at too high a temperature, it can become tough and crumbly.

While the tofu is heating, ask your guests to pour some of the warm sauce into their individual bowls and then to flavour the sauce with their selection of the condiments.

Use a slotted spoon to transfer the tofu into the bowls with the sauce. This dish makes up the centrepiece of a great winter dinner—simply accompany with various side dishes.

simmered tofu

sukiyaki

600 g (1 lb 5 oz) beef sirloin with fat
250 g (9 oz) fresh shirataki noodles or
100 g (3½ oz) dried harusame noodles
8 fresh shiitake mushrooms, stems discarded
and a cross cut into the top of each cap
2 baby leeks or 4 spring onions (scallions),
cut into 2 cm (¾ in) slices on the
diagonal
¼ Chinese cabbage, cut into 3 cm (1¼ in)
wide sections (keep the layers together)
300 g (10½ oz) firm tofu, cut into 3 cm
(1¼ in) cubes

4 small eggs
15 g (½ oz) mitsuba or flat-leaf (Italian)
parsley

SAUCE
500 ml (2 cups) dashi II (page 245)
125 ml (½ cup) Japanese soy sauce
80 ml (⅓ cup) mirin
1½ tablespoons sake
2 tablespoons sugar

Serves 4 as a main

Trim the fat off the beef and cut the fat into squares. Freeze the beef for 3 hours, or until partially frozen. Meanwhile, soak the shirataki noodles in boiling water for 2 minutes (if using harusame, soak for 10 minutes in hot water). Drain well and cut into 5 cm (2 in) lengths. Using a very sharp knife, cut the beef along its length, as thinly as you can, to form long, thin strips (or ask a butcher to do this for you). Put on a large serving platter with the vegetables, tofu, beef fat, noodles and mitsuba in their separate groups. Cover and refrigerate.

To make the sauce, combine all the ingredients in a saucepan and bring to the boil, then pour into a vessel with a pouring lip just prior to eating.

Set up a shallow cast-iron or flameproof casserole dish over a gas burner or electric hotplate on the table. Put an empty platter next to it and ask your guests to crack an egg into a small bowl, which they keep nearby. Melt some of the beef fat in the dish over medium–high heat and rub over the base.

Lightly brown the leek, then the beef in batches, then transfer to the empty platter. Melt a little more fat if needed, then add half of each vegetable (including the leek) and enough sauce just to cover. Allow to come to a simmer, then cook for about 5 minutes, or until just tender. Make space for the beef and add half to the dish and cook for another minute, or until it is just heated through, adding half the mitsuba in the last few seconds.

Ask guests to help themselves and dip each cooked ingredient into the egg if they wish—the residual heat will cook the egg. Repeat the cooking process with the remaining ingredients, adding more water if needed. Serve with rice.

500 g (1 lb 2 oz) sirloin steak, trimmed
550 g (2½ cups) Japanese short-grain rice
375 ml (1½ cups) dashi II (page 245)
80 ml (⅓ cup) Japanese soy sauce
60 ml (¼ cup) mirin
2 teaspoons caster (superfine) sugar
1 small onion, very thinly sliced
10 g (¼ oz) mitsuba or flat-leaf
   (Italian) parsley
4 eggs, lightly beaten

Serves 4 as a main

Freeze the beef for 3 hours, or until partially frozen. Use a sharp knife to slice very thinly along the length of the steak to form long, thin strips.

Meanwhile, rinse the rice several times in cold water until the water runs clear, then drain in a colander for 1 hour. Put in a saucepan with 750 ml (3 cups) water. Bring to the boil, then cover with a tight-fitting lid, reduce the heat to low and simmer for 15 minutes. Turn off the heat but leave the pan on the hotplate. Working quickly, remove the lid, lay a clean tea towel over the top, then put the lid on and allow to stand for 15 minutes.

Pour the dashi, soy sauce and mirin into a large saucepan, add the sugar and bring to the boil over high heat. Add the onion, allow to come to the boil again, then cook for 3 minutes, or until tender. Add the meat and allow the liquid to just return to the boil, then reduce to a simmer and cook for about 2–3 minutes, separating with chopsticks to promote even cooking, until the meat changes colour and is just cooked through.

Scatter the mitsuba over the top, then quickly pour the eggs over in a circular motion and cook for about 1 minute, or until the egg is just starting to set. Turn off the heat, cover with a lid and sit for a further 2–3 minutes, or until the egg is half set. Divide the hot rice among four wide, deep bowls, then spoon the beef mixture over the top of them—the hot rice will continue to cook the egg.

beef and rice bowl

glazed beef
and vegetable rolls

400 g (14 oz) sirloin steak (3 cm/
1¼ in thick), trimmed
2½ teaspoons potato starch, for sprinkling
6 spring onions (scallions), cut into
12 x 6 cm (2½ in) lengths
6 thin asparagus spears, trimmed, cut in
half and lightly blanched

vegetable oil, for cooking
80 ml (⅓ cup) sake
80 ml (⅓ cup) mirin
80 ml (⅓ cup) Japanese soy sauce
1½ tablespoons caster (superfine) sugar

Makes 12 rolls

Freeze the beef for 3 hours, or until partially frozen. Use a sharp knife to slice very thinly along the length of the steak to form long, thin strips—you should have about 24 slices. Lay one strip of beef on a very clean workbench with the short end towards you. Lay another strip alongside it so that it just overlaps along its length, forming one strip of meat about 6 cm (2½ in) wide at the short end. Sprinkle with a little seasoned potato starch. Repeat with the rest of the meat—you should have 12 strips in total. Put a piece of spring onion and asparagus along the edge of the beef closest to you, then roll up and secure with kitchen string. Repeat with the remaining beef and vegetables.

Heat a little vegetable oil in a large frying pan over medium–high heat, then, working in batches, cook the rolls for 5–7 minutes, or until browned all over. Remove from the pan.

Combine the sake, mirin, soy sauce and sugar with 80 ml (⅓ cup) water, then add to the pan, stirring until the sugar dissolves. Bring to the boil for 1 minute, then reduce to a simmer. Add the beef rolls and cook for 5 minutes, or until cooked through, turning occasionally. Remove from the pan and set aside.

Carefully cut the string from the rolls, then cover the rolls with foil and set aside until needed. Pour any meat juices into the pan, then sit the pan over medium–high heat and bring to the boil. Cook for 5–7 minutes, or until the liquid is slightly thickened and glossy. Immediately return the beef rolls to the pan and cook for a further minute, turning continuously to coat and glaze well. Remove from the heat (cut each roll into thirds if serving with chopsticks) and drizzle with the remaining glaze before serving immediately. Great with a crisp green salad and a bowl of rice.

festival foods... There are thousands of festivals celebrated all over Japan every year. Although a few of these celebrations are secular, most are a form of Shinto worship called *matsuri,* while others are, or once were, rites of Buddhism. Festival foods are divided into two types: food for the people and food for the gods.

The Japanese year begins with the biggest and most elaborate festival of all, *O-Shogatsu,* and the traditional foods associated with this celebration are rife with symbolism. The length of *toshikoshi soba,* literally 'year-crossing buckwheat noodles' symbolizes long life and a smooth transition from one year to the next. *Osechi ryori* consists of dozens of kinds of small delicacies artfully arranged in exquisite lacquered boxes. Most of these foods have word, shape or colour associations with happiness, good fortune, good health, prosperity, peace, long life, fertility and abundance, so with each bite these hopes are internalized.

Other festivals also have certain food associations; for example, the spring festival of *Setsubun* where dried soya beans are scattered in homes to chase away demons, or Girls' Day when *sekihan,* glutinous rice studded with red *azuki* beans, is the celebratory dish. Pink *sakura mochi,* a rice confection wrapped in a cherry leaf, is a favourite treat of cherry blossom season.

The gods are fed daily with the basic Shinto offerings of uncooked rice, *sake* and salt. At festival time, fruits, vegetables, fish, seaweed and even confections — the finest 'fruits' of land and sea — are added upon shrine altars, sometimes in truly extravagant quantities. Once the gods have consumed their essence, they are sometimes distributed to worshippers to take home or they may be prepared at the shrine itself for a communal post-festival meal called *naorai*. Nor are the dead forgotten. Particularly during the *O-Bon* festival, the spirits of ancestors and late loved ones are offered a variety of foods.

60 ml (¼ cup) Japanese soy sauce
2 tablespoons mirin
2 tablespoons sake
1½ tablespoons caster (superfine) sugar
2 teaspoons vegetable oil
4 x 200 g (7 oz) chicken thigh fillets with
**   skin, or cutlets, with the bone removed**

Serves 4 as a main

Combine the soy sauce, mirin, sake and sugar in a small bowl and stir until the sugar has dissolved. Set aside.

Heat the oil in a large, heavy-based frying pan over medium–high heat, then add the chicken, skin-side down, and cook for 4–5 minutes, or until the skin is golden. Turn over and cook for a further 3–4 minutes, or until golden and the chicken is almost cooked through. Remove from the pan.

Discard any excess fat from the pan, then pour in the soy mixture, increase the heat to high and bring to the boil. Cook for 1 minute, or until the liquid is slightly reduced and glossy. Return the chicken and any juices to the pan and turn to coat well. Remove from the pan and slice on a slight angle into 1.5 cm (⅝ in) wide strips. Holding the fillets in their original shape, transfer to a plate and accompany with rice and vegetables or a salad.

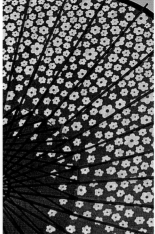

teriyaki chicken

sautéed pork and cabbage

500 g (1 lb 2 oz) pork loin fillet, cut into
    15–20 cm (6–8 in) lengths
1 tablespoon vegetable oil
2 teaspoons sesame oil
4 spring onions (scallions), cut into
    3 cm (1¼ in) lengths
250 g (9 oz) Chinese cabbage, cut
    lengthways into 2 cm (¾ in)
    wide strips
60 ml (¼ cup) Japanese soy sauce
1 tablespoon mirin
125 ml (½ cup) dashi II (page 245)
3 teaspoons finely grated fresh ginger
    and its juice
2 garlic cloves, crushed
1 teaspoon caster (superfine) sugar
large pinch of ground white pepper

Serves 4 as a main

Freeze the pork for 3 hours, or until partially frozen. Use a sharp knife to slice very thinly along the length of the fillet to form long, thin strips.

Heat half the vegetable and sesame oils in a large frying pan over medium–high heat. Working in batches, cook the pork strips for 10 seconds on each side, using more oil as needed. Remove and set aside.

Add the spring onion and cabbage to the pan and stir-fry for 1 minute, or until softened. Combine the soy sauce, mirin, dashi, ginger and ginger juice, garlic, sugar and white pepper, add to the pan and bring to the boil. Return the pork to the pan and cook for a further 1–2 minutes, or until the pork is cooked through and tender. Serve immediately with rice.

500 g (1 lb 2 oz) sirloin steak, trimmed
2 large all-purpose potatoes, cut into
   3 cm (1¼ in) pieces
1 tablespoon sesame oil
60 ml (¼ cup) vegetable oil
1 large onion, cut in half, then sliced into
   1 cm (½ in) wide wedges

375 ml (1½ cups) dashi II (page 245)
80 ml (⅓ cup) Japanese soy sauce
2 tablespoons black or dark brown sugar
60 ml (¼ cup) sake

Serves 4 as a main

Freeze the beef for 3 hours, or until partially frozen. Meanwhile, soak the potato in cold water for 30 minutes, then drain well.

Use a sharp knife to slice the steak very thinly along its length to form long, thin strips. Cut the strips into 4 cm (1½ in) lengths. Combine the steak with the sesame oil and 1 tablespoon of the vegetable oil until well coated.

Heat a large saucepan over medium–high heat, then add a little of the remaining oil and the potato and cook for 8 minutes, or until lightly browned all over. Remove from the pan and set aside. Pour in a little more oil, then add the onions and cook for 5 minutes, or until lightly golden. Set aside with the potatoes.

Add half the beef strips to the pan and quickly separate and turn with chopsticks for 3–5 minutes, or until the meat just changes colour, then set aside. Repeat with the remaining beef.

Return the potato, onion and beef to the pan along with the dashi, soy sauce, sugar and sake and bring to the boil. Reduce to a simmer and cook for 30–45 minutes, or until the meat and potatoes are tender, but not falling apart. Season to taste. The liquid should still be brothy.

Serve the solid ingredients in a bowl and spoon over a little of the broth.

beef and
potato stew

chicken wing
and soya bean stew

300 g (1½ cups) dried soya beans
1 kg (2 lb 4 oz) chicken wings
2 teaspoons sesame oil
4–5 baby leeks (white part only), cut into
**   3 cm (1¼ in) pieces**
1 tablespoon finely grated fresh ginger
125 ml (½ cup) Japanese soy sauce
60 ml (¼ cup) mirin
60 ml (¼ cup) sake
1 tablespoon caster (superfine) sugar
Japanese mustard, to serve, optional

Serves 4 as a main

Soak the soya beans in cold water overnight. Rinse well and put in a saucepan with enough water to cover. Bring to the boil over high heat, then reduce to a simmer for about 3 hours, or until tender, topping up with water as needed. Remove any scum that forms on the surface as the beans cook. Drain, reserving the cooking liquid.

Meanwhile, remove and discard the tips from the chicken wings, then cut in half at the joint.

Heat the sesame oil in a large saucepan over high heat. Cook the chicken wings in two batches for about 5 minutes per batch, or until golden. Set aside. Drain most of the oil from the pan, leaving about 1 tablespoon in the pan.

Add the leek to the pan and cook for 2 minutes, or until lightly golden. Add the ginger and stir for a few seconds before returning the chicken wings to the pan, along with the beans and enough of the reserved cooking liquid to cover. Top up with cold water if needed.

Add the soy sauce, mirin, sake and sugar and bring to the boil. Reduce to a simmer and cook for about 20 minutes, or until the chicken is almost cooked through. Increase the heat to high and boil for about 20 minutes, or until the liquid reduces and thickens slightly. Pour into a serving dish and, if you like, serve with Japanese mustard. This dish is great served with rice and some lightly cooked green vegetables.

25 g (1 oz) butter
1 teaspoon sesame oil
2 tablespoons vegetable oil
1 large onion, cut in half, then sliced into
  1 cm (½ in) wedges
750 g (1 lb 10 oz) pork or lamb shoulder
  or chuck steak, cut into 3 cm (1¼ in)
  cubes
pinch of ground white pepper
2 garlic cloves, crushed
1½ tablespoons Japanese curry powder
375 ml (1½ cups) dashi II (page 245)

2 tablespoons mirin
1 tablespoon Japanese soy sauce
3 tablespoons white miso
2 large all-purpose potatoes, cut into
  2 cm (¾ in) cubes
2 carrots, cut in half lengthways, then cut
  into 3 cm (1¼ in) pieces
100 g (3½ oz) green beans, trimmed and
  cut into 4 cm (1½ in) lengths
pickles, to serve

Serves 4 as a main

Heat the butter, sesame oil and half the vegetable oil in a large saucepan over medium heat, then add the onion and cook, stirring regularly, for 10–15 minutes, or until golden. Remove from the pan and set aside.

Pour the remaining vegetable oil into the pan. Season the meat with salt and white pepper, then cook it in batches for 5–7 minutes, or until browned all over. Remove from the pan and set aside.

Add the garlic and curry powder to the pan and stir for 1 minute, or until fragrant. Return the onion and meat to the pan and stir to coat with the curry. Pour in the dashi, mirin, soy sauce and 500 ml (2 cups) water, then stir in the miso. Bring to the boil, then reduce to a simmer and cook for 1 hour. Add the potato and carrot and cook for a further 50 minutes. Add the beans and cook for 10 minutes, or until everything is very tender. Season to taste and serve over rice or noodles, accompanied by pickles of your choice.

黄金らっき

japanese curry

chicken and vegetable hotpot

100 g (3½ oz) gobo (burdock root)
1 teaspoon Japanese rice vinegar
100 g (3½ oz) lotus root
2 teaspoons sesame oil
1 tablespoon vegetable oil
750 g (1 lb 10 oz) chicken thigh fillets,
    cut into 3 cm (1¼ in) squares
150 g (5½ oz) taro, peeled and cut into
    2 cm (¾ in) squares
1 carrot, cut on the diagonal into 1.5 cm
    (⅝ in) thick slices
100 g (3½ oz) sliced bamboo shoots

100 g (3½ oz) fresh shiitake mushrooms,
    stems discarded, large caps halved
500 ml (2 cups) dashi II (page 245)
80 ml (⅓ cup) Japanese soy sauce
60 ml (¼ cup) mirin
1 tablespoon caster (superfine) sugar
100 g (3½ oz) snow peas (mangetout),
    trimmed
shichimi togarashi (seven spice mix),
    optional

Serves 4 as a main or 8 as a side

Roughly scrape the skin of the gobo with a sharp knife, then rinse. Cut into 2 cm (¾ in) pieces on the diagonal. Put in a bowl with 500 ml (2 cups) water and the rice vinegar. Leave for about 15 minutes to remove some of the bitterness from the gobo. Drain well.

If you are using fresh lotus, peel it, cut into 5 mm (¼ in) slices, then put in cold water.

Heat the sesame and vegetable oils in a large saucepan over medium–high heat and cook the chicken in batches until lightly golden. Remove from the pan and set aside.

Drain the gobo and lotus. Add the gobo and taro to the pan and cook, stirring frequently for 2 minutes. Now add the lotus and carrot and cook for a further 2 minutes, or until lightly golden. Add the bamboo and shiitake and cook a further 2 minutes. Pour in the dashi, soy sauce and mirin, add the sugar and bring to the boil, then reduce to a simmer and add the chicken and simmer for a further 10–15 minutes. Just before serving, add the snow peas and stir until just wilted. Serve in deep bowls with rice. Sprinkle with shichimi togarashi, if desired.

2 teaspoons vegetable oil
1 kg (2 lb 4 oz) boneless pork belly, cut
into 5 cm (2 in) cubes
100 g (3½ oz) fresh ginger, peeled and cut
into thick slices
500 ml (2 cups) dashi II (page 245)
170 ml (⅔ cup) sake
60 ml (¼ cup) mirin
80 g (⅓ cup) firmly packed black or dark
brown sugar
125 ml (½ cup) Japanese soy sauce
Japanese mustard, to serve, optional

Serves 4–6 as a main

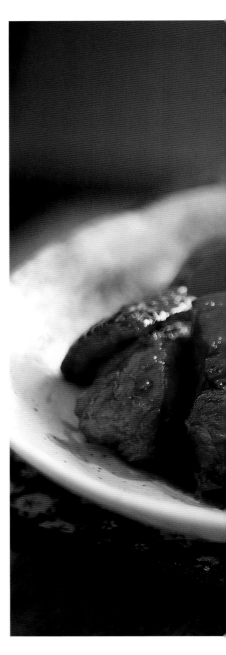

Heat the vegetable oil in a large, heavy-based saucepan or small flameproof casserole dish over high heat. Add the pork in two batches and cook the pork pieces for 5 minutes, or until browned all over.

Rinse the pork under hot water to remove excess oil. Remove any excess fat from the pan and return the pork to the pan, adding enough cold water to cover well. Add the ginger slices and bring to the boil over high heat. Reduce to a simmer and cook for 2 hours. Top up with water if needed. Strain, discarding the liquid and ginger. Set the pork aside.

Put the dashi, sake, mirin, sugar and soy sauce in a clean heavy-based saucepan and stir over high heat until the sugar has dissolved. Add the pork and return to the boil, then reduce to a simmer and cook, turning occasionally, for 1 hour, or until the pork is very tender. Remove from the heat and allow the pork to rest in the liquid for 20 minutes. Place the pork in a serving dish, cover and keep warm while you reduce the sauce.

Sit the saucepan over high heat, bring the liquid to the boil and cook for 5 minutes, or until the sauce has reduced to a slightly syrupy glaze. Return the pork to the sauce and stir to combine before arranging in a serving dish. Pour over any remaining sauce and serve immediately, with a little Japanese mustard on the side if using. It's also great served with rice and Asian greens.

okinawan slow-cooked pork

simmered chicken meatballs

300 g (10½ oz) chicken thigh fillets
2 spring onions (scallions), chopped
1 teaspoon finely grated fresh ginger
   and its juice
1 egg
1 teaspoon sake
1 tablespoon Japanese soy sauce
1 teaspoon mirin
20 g (⅓ cup) panko (Japanese
   breadcrumbs)
1 teaspoon sesame oil
1 tablespoon vegetable oil

SAUCE
500 ml (2 cups) dashi II (page 245)
80 ml (⅓ cup) mirin
60 ml (¼ cup) sake
4 cm (1½ in) length of konbu, wiped with
   a damp cloth and cut into 1 cm
   (½ in) strips
1½ tablespoons Japanese soy sauce
1 teaspoon kuzu starch or arrowroot

thinly sliced spring onion (scallion) or
   nori strips, for garnish, optional

Serves 4 as a main

Put the chicken in a food processor and process until roughly minced (ground). Add the spring onion, ginger and ginger juice, egg, sake, soy sauce and mirin and process until finely chopped. Turn out into a bowl and add the breadcrumbs, mixing well with clean hands to combine. Cover and refrigerate for 1 hour. Roll into balls 3 cm (1¼ in) in diameter.

Heat the sesame and vegetable oils in a non-stick frying pan over medium heat and add the balls in batches. Cook for 5 minutes, or until lightly golden all over. Remove the pan from the heat.

Combine all the sauce ingredients except the kuzu in a saucepan and bring to the boil over high heat. Remove the konbu and discard. Add the chicken balls and return the sauce to the boil, then reduce to a simmer and cook for 5 minutes, or until they are cooked through. Remove the meatballs with a slotted spoon and set aside.

Mix the kuzu with a little of the hot liquid in a small bowl, until a loose paste is formed, then stir into the pan—stir over high heat until the sauce boils and thickens to a light coating consistency. Place the balls in a serving bowl and pour the sauce over. If you like, garnish with spring onion or nori strips.

soy

Japanese cuisine would certainly not be what it is without the ubiquitous soya bean. Called *daizu*, this versatile and nutritious legume makes its way into nearly every meal in one or more forms. *Edamame*, green soya beans boiled and shelled, are a popular hot weather accompaniment to beer or *sake*. Dried yellow soya beans, soaked and boiled, are added to many different dishes.

The beans are pressed for their oil, as well as roasted and ground into *kinako* powder, a popular coating for rice cakes and dumplings. Cooked with water, the beans produce soy milk. The skin formed on the surface of heated soy milk is called *yuba*, and *yuba* is itself prepared in many different ways,

particularly in Kyoto. The versatile bean curd called *tofu* is made by heating soy milk with a coagulant.

Soy sauce, fermented from soya beans, wheat, water and salt, is a basic condiment in the Japanese kitchen and sometimes at the table. *Miso* also figures largely in Japanese cooking and is made by fermenting soya beans, usually in combination with another grain, such as rice or barley.

And then, of course, there is *natto*, fermented soya beans, whose strong aroma and flavour, as well as sticky texture, are an acquired taste, and one that rarely seems to find appreciation outside of Japan.

2 litres (8 cups) dashi II (page 245)
1 carrot, peeled and chopped
1 celery stalk, chopped
6 spring onions (scallions)
10 x 2 cm (4 x ¾ in) piece of fresh ginger,
    thickly sliced
1 kg (2 lb 4 oz) pork loin fillet

SALAD
2 Lebanese (short) cucumbers
12 cm (5 in) length of daikon, peeled
1 celery stalk
3 spring onions (scallions)

SAUCE
2 tablespoons red miso
2 tablespoons white miso
2 tablespoons sake
1 teaspoon sesame oil
2 tablespoons caster (superfine) sugar
2 garlic cloves, crushed

Serves 4 as a main

Combine the dashi, carrot, celery, spring onion and ginger in a saucepan just large enough to fit the piece of pork. Sit the pan over high heat and bring the liquid to the boil. Meanwhile, tie the pork with string to help it keep its shape.

Lower the pork into the stock, return the stock to the boil, then reduce to a simmer and cook, turning the pork occasionally, for 40–45 minutes, or until evenly cooked through and tender. Remove the pan from the heat and allow the pork to cool slightly in the liquid. Transfer the pork to a bowl, then strain the stock on top. Cover and refrigerate until chilled.

To make the salad, cut the cucumber, daikon, celery and spring onion into 6 cm (2½ in) lengths, then cut into thin strips or julienne.

Remove the pork from the liquid and reserve 60 ml (¼ cup) of the poaching liquid. Freeze the remaining liquid for use as a soup base or discard.

To make the sauce, combine all the ingredients and the reserved poaching liquid into a small bowl and stir until smooth.

Slice the pork, then serve over the salad with sauce drizzled over or to the side.

poached pork
with miso sauce

chicken hotpot

10 x 10 cm (4 x 4 in) piece of konbu,
    wiped with a damp cloth and cut into
    1 cm (½ in) wide strips
1.5 kg (3 lb 5 oz) whole chicken, cut into
    5 cm (2 in) pieces
1 carrot, peeled, cut into 5 mm (¼ in) slices
100 g (3½ oz) harusame (bean thread
    noodles)
150 g (5½ oz) fresh shiitake mushrooms,
    stems discarded
300 g (10½ oz) firm tofu, cut into
    3 cm (1¼ oz) cubes
4 baby leeks, cut into 3 cm (1¼ in) lengths
    on the diagonal

¼ Chinese cabbage, cut into bite-sized chunks
100 g (3½ oz) tinned bamboo shoots,
    cut into 5 mm (¼ in) thick slices
50 g (1¾ oz) mitsuba, cut into 2 cm
    (¾ in) lengths
1 quantity ponzu (page 246) or 250 ml
    (1 cup) ready-made

CONDIMENTS
70 g (2½ oz) daikon, peeled, finely grated,
    then squeezed to remove excess liquid
thinly sliced spring onions (scallions)

Serves 4 as a main

Soak the konbu for an hour in a large saucepan of cold water. Put the pan over high heat and bring to the boil. Remove the konbu strips. Add the chicken pieces, return to the boil, then reduce to a simmer and cook for about 10 minutes, removing the chicken pieces as they are just cooked. Pour a little of the stock over the cooked chicken to keep it moist. Add the carrot to the stock and cook for 1 minute, then remove with a slotted spoon and set aside. Strain the stock and pour into a *nabe* (cooking pot) or flameproof casserole dish until it reaches halfway up the sides. Freeze the rest of the broth.

Soak the noodles in hot water for 10 minutes, then drain well. Set aside. Cut a small cross in the mushroom caps. Arrange the chicken on a platter and the noodles, tofu and all the vegetables and mitsuba on a separate platter and take to the table. Give each person a small bowl of ponzu for dipping and allow them to mix in daikon and spring onions to taste.

Bring the stock to a simmer over a portable gas burner or electric hotplate set in the middle of the table. Cook half of each ingredient for 5–7 minutes, or until heated through and tender. Each person should remove a little of each ingredient from the pot with chopsticks and dip into their sauce. When the first batch of ingredients has been removed from the stock, cook the remaining ingredients. If the stock gets a little low, you can top it up with boiling water. Alternatively, cook the hotpot on the stovetop and bring the pot to the table. Serve with rice.

45 g (1 cup) finely shredded Chinese
   cabbage
250 g (2 cups) plain (all-purpose) flour
50 g (¼ cup) potato starch
½ teaspoon baking powder
170 ml (⅔ cup) dashi II (page 245)
1 tablespoon white miso
1 tablespoon mirin
3 eggs, lightly beaten
4 fresh shiitake mushrooms, thinly sliced
4 spring onions (scallions), thinly sliced
1 tablespoon finely chopped pickled ginger
300 g (10½ oz) raw seafood or meat, or
   vegetables, chopped into small pieces
pinch of ground white pepper
vegetable oil, for cooking
sesame oil, for cooking

SAUCE
60 ml (¼ cup) tomato sauce (ketchup)
2½ tablespoons Japanese soy sauce
1 tablespoon sake
1 tablespoon mirin
1½ tablespoons caster (superfine) sugar
2 tablespoons Japanese rice vinegar
1 teaspoon finely grated fresh ginger
1 garlic clove, crushed
¼ teaspoon Japanese mustard

CONDIMENTS
Japanese mayonnaise
nori strips or flakes
fine katsuobushi (bonito flakes)

Serves 4 as a main

Sprinkle the cabbage with salt, stand for 5 minutes, then squeeze out any excess liquid.

Sift the flour, potato starch and baking powder into a bowl. Combine the dashi, miso and mirin in a separate bowl and whisk until smooth. Make a well in the centre of the flour and add the egg and the dashi mixture and mix to combine. Stir in the cabbage, shiitake, spring onion, pickled ginger and your choice of seafood, meat or vegetables, then season with salt and white pepper.

Heat a little of the vegetable and sesame oils in a large frying pan over medium heat and add one-quarter of the mixture. Cook for 5 minutes, or until bubbles appear on the surface. Turn over and cook for a further 5 minutes, or until cooked through. Keep warm in a low oven. Repeat with the remaining batter.

To make the sauce, combine all the ingredients in a small saucepan with 2 tablespoons water and bring to the boil over high heat, then reduce to a simmer and cook, stirring, for 10 minutes, or until slightly thickened.

Brush the top of the pancake with the sauce. Serve with the condiments and some extra sauce in a small bowl with a spoon for drizzling over the top.

savoury pancake

fried pork cutlet

4 x 150 g (5½ oz) pork schnitzels or
   700 g (1 lb 9 oz) pork fillets
plain (all-purpose) flour, for dusting
1 egg, lightly beaten
panko (Japanese breadcrumbs), for coating
vegetable oil, for deep-frying
60 ml (¼ cup) sesame oil
¼ white cabbage, very finely shredded
lemon wedges, to serve
Japanese mustard, to serve, optional

TONKATSU SAUCE
60 ml (¼ cup) Worcestershire sauce
2 tablespoons tamari or
   Japanese soy sauce
2 tablespoons caster (superfine) sugar
2 tablespoons tomato sauce (ketchup)
½ teaspoon Japanese mustard
1 tablespoon sake
1 tablespoon Japanese rice vinegar
1 garlic clove, bruised

Serves 4 as a main

Using a meat mallet or back of a large, heavy knife, pound the pork schnitzel until 5 mm (¼ in) thick, then lightly score around the edges with the point of the knife to prevent it from curling during cooking. If using pork fillets, trim off any skinny ends and cut into 5 cm (2 in) lengths—do not pound.

Lightly coat the pork in seasoned flour. Dip the pork pieces into the egg, allowing any excess to drip off, then coat in the panko, pressing down on either side to help the crumbs adhere. Put on a plate, cover and refrigerate for 15 minutes.

Meanwhile, to make the sauce, combine all the ingredients in a small saucepan and bring to the boil over high heat, then reduce to a simmer and cook for 20 minutes, or until glossy and thickened slightly.

Fill a deep heavy-based saucepan or deep-fat fryer one-third full of vegetable oil and add the sesame oil. Heat to 170°C (325°F), or until a cube of bread dropped into the oil browns in 20 seconds. Cook the schnitzels one at a time, or the fillet a few pieces at a time, turning once or twice for about 4 minutes, or until golden brown all over and cooked through. The fillet will take a little longer, about 6–8 minutes. Drain on crumpled paper towel, then keep warm in a low oven while you cook the rest.

Slice the pork schnitzel, then lift it onto serving plates in its original shape, accompanied by a pile of cabbage and lemon wedges, and pass around the sauce. If you like, serve with mustard. For a hearty meal serve with rice, miso soup (page 145) and pickles.

a little taste of...

When the sixteenth-century Japanese first saw *namban ryori,* the cuisine of the 'southern barbarians' (the Portuguese who arrived by southern routes), they were revolted. So too were their descendants when a long-isolated Japan opened its doors to Americans and Europeans several centuries later. Despite this initial reaction, the Japanese are known for their inclination to adapt foreign things to their own tastes, and the Meiji era of the late nineteenth and early twentieth centuries was to become the heyday of tasting and transformation. *Yoshoku* means 'Western food' but it actually refers to those early dishes that the Japanese adapted to suit themselves. Among them are *omuraisu,* an omelette wrapped around flavoured rice. Unique versions of Western foods continue to appear, such as spaghetti tossed with cod roe and seaweed, or pizza topped with corn and mayonnaise. And bread, introduced to Japan by the Portuguese so long ago, is often transformed into surprising creations, such as *yakisoba* pastry topped with dried fish flakes, or sandwiches filled with potato salad or a combination of cream and fruit.

...yoshoku

tomato and tofu salad

3 vine-ripened tomatoes
200 g (7 oz) mizuna or 100 g (3½ oz)
   baby rocket (arugula)
200 g (7 oz) silken firm tofu
1 toasted nori sheet

DRESSING
1 tablespoon Japanese soy sauce
1½ tablespoons Japanese rice vinegar
1 teaspoon sesame oil
1 tablespoon vegetable oil
1 small garlic clove, crushed
1 teaspoon finely grated fresh ginger
1 teaspoon mirin
1 teaspoon caster (superfine) sugar
¼ teaspoon Japanese mustard

Serves 6–8 as a side

Cut each tomato into six wedges. Rinse the mizuna, shake out the excess water and cut into 3 cm (1¼ in) lengths. Cut the tofu into 2 cm (¾ in) dice.

Using scissors cut the toasted nori sheet into thin strips, 3 cm x 5 mm (1¼ x ¼ in).

To make the dressing, combine all the ingredients in a bowl and whisk until smooth. (This dressing is also great served over a green salad.)

Gently toss the tomatoes and mizuna together and place in a serving bowl. Distribute the tofu over the top and pour over the dressing. Sprinkle with the nori strips and serve immediately.

200 g (7 oz) Chinese cabbage
1 carrot, peeled
150 g (5½ oz) daikon, peeled
2 spring onions (scallions)
2 teaspoons black sesame seeds, toasted

DRESSING
125 g (½ cup) Japanese mayonnaise
1½ tablespoons Japanese rice vinegar
1 tablespoon sake
¼ teaspoon Japanese mustard or
   wasabi paste
½ teaspoon sesame oil
2 teaspoons Japanese soy sauce
1 teaspoon caster (superfine) sugar
ground white pepper

Serves 6–8 as a side

Finely shred the cabbage and put in a large bowl. Cut the carrot and daikon into 5 cm (2 in) lengths, then julienne using a Japanese mandolin with the coarse-tooth comb, or coarsely grate. Place the daikon in a colander, sprinkle with salt and allow to sit for 15 minutes. Squeeze out any excess moisture with your hands.

Meanwhile, to make the dressing, put all the ingredients in a bowl and mix until smooth. Season to taste with salt and ground white pepper.

Add the daikon and carrot to the cabbage. Thinly slice the spring onions on the diagonal and add to the cabbage, along with the sesame seeds and the dressing. Toss well, then serve.

japanese coleslaw

japanese
potato salad

500 g (1 lb 2 oz) all-purpose potatoes,
   peeled
50 g (1¾ oz) sliced ham
1 Lebanese (short) cucumber
extra mitsuba leaves, to garnish, optional

DRESSING
185 g (¾ cup) Japanese mayonnaise
½ teaspoon Japanese mustard
2 tablespoons Japanese rice vinegar
a few drops of sesame oil
2 spring onions (scallions), finely chopped
25 g (¾ cup) finely chopped mitsuba
   leaves
ground white pepper

Serves 6–8 as a side

Cut the potatoes into 2 cm (¾ in) dice. Bring a saucepan of salted water to the boil and add the potato. Cook for 8–10 minutes, or until tender. Drain, rinse under cold running water, then drain again. Crush the potatoes lightly with a fork but do not mash—there should still be some lumps.

Meanwhile, cut the ham into thin strips, about 3 cm (1¼ in) in length. Cut the cucumber in half lengthways and scoop out the seeds with a teaspoon, then slice very thinly.

To make the dressing, combine the mayonnaise, mustard, vinegar and sesame oil until smooth, then stir in the spring onion and chopped mitsuba. Season with salt and ground white pepper.

Put the warm potato, ham, cucumber and dressing in a bowl and toss to combine well. Allow to sit for 15 minutes so the potato can absorb some of the dressing and the flavours can develop. Serve in a bowl garnished with extra mitsuba leaves, if desired.

750 ml (3 cups) dashi II (page 245)
2 x 250 g (9 oz) chicken breast fillets, skinless
155 g (5½ oz) asparagus, cut into 3 cm (1¼ in) lengths on the diagonal
1 Lebanese (short) cucumber, cut in half lengthways
1 baby cos (romaine) lettuce, cut into bite-sized pieces
325 g (11½ oz) mizuna or 150 g (5½ oz) baby English spinach, cut into 3 cm (1¼ in) lengths
40 g (⅓ cup) walnuts, toasted
200 g (7 oz) small rice crackers or larger ones broken up

DRESSING
2 tablespoons finely grated daikon, squeezed to remove excess liquid
1 tablespoon Japanese soy sauce
1 tablespoon mirin
3½ tablespoons Japanese rice vinegar
½ teaspoon finely grated fresh ginger
1 garlic clove, crushed
½ teaspoon sesame oil
1 tablespoon vegetable oil
1 teaspoon sugar

Serves 4 as a main or 8 as a starter

Pour the dashi into a deep frying pan over high heat and bring to the boil. Add the chicken breasts and return to the boil. Reduce to a simmer for 12 minutes, then cover and turn off the heat. Rest for 30 minutes. Transfer the chicken and cooking liquid to a bowl and refrigerate for 1½ hours, or until cold. Drain, reserving 1 tablespoon of the cooking liquid for the dressing (use the rest for a soup base or discard) and slice or shred the chicken.

Meanwhile, bring a small saucepan of water to the boil and cook the asparagus for 1 minute, or until just tender. Rinse, then plunge into iced water. Using a teaspoon, scoop the seeds from the cucumber, then thinly slice the flesh on the diagonal.

To make the dressing, combine all the ingredients and the reserved cooking liquid in a small bowl and whisk until smooth.

Combine the chicken with the dressing. Put the asparagus, cucumber, lettuce, mizuna and walnuts in a bowl and toss to combine. Add the chicken and dressing and toss again. Place on a serving platter and sprinkle over the rice crackers. Serve immediately.

chicken and cracker salad

japanese hamburger

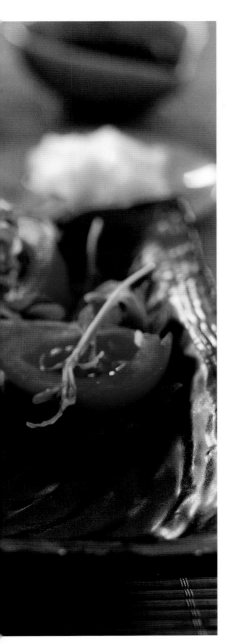

150 g (5½ oz) silken firm tofu
300 g (10½ oz) minced (ground) pork
300 g (10½ oz) minced (ground) beef
1 small onion, finely chopped
60 g (1 cup) panko (Japanese breadcrumbs)
2 tablespoons Japanese soy sauce
1 tablespoon mirin
2 garlic cloves, crushed
3 teaspoons finely grated fresh ginger

1 egg, lightly beaten
ground white pepper
3 tablespoons finely grated daikon, squeezed to extract any excess liquid
1 teaspoon finely grated fresh ginger, extra
vegetable oil, for pan-frying
Japanese soy sauce, for drizzling

Serves 4 as a main

To weight the tofu, wrap it in a clean tea towel. Put two plates on top of the tofu and leave for about 1 hour to extract any excess moisture. Remove from the tea towel, then pat dry with paper towels. Transfer to a bowl and finely mash with a fork.

Add the pork, beef, onion, panko, soy sauce, mirin, garlic, ginger and egg to the bowl and combine well. Season with salt and ground white pepper. Refrigerate for 2 hours. Shape into eight oval patties about 2 cm (¾ in) thick. Set aside.

Combine the daikon and extra ginger.

Heat a little oil in large non-stick frying pan over medium–high heat and cook the patties in batches for 7–8 minutes on each side, or until cooked through. Top the patties with a little mound of the daikon mixture and drizzle with soy sauce. Serve immediately. Great accompanied with rice and salad.

600 g (1 lb 5 oz) block firm (cotton) tofu
25 g (1 oz) butter
1 teaspoon sesame oil
2 garlic cloves, crushed
2 teaspoons finely grated fresh ginger
4 spring onions (scallions), sliced on the
    diagonal into 4 cm (1½ in) lengths
150 g (5½ oz) shimeji mushrooms, pulled
    apart in small clumps
150 g (5½ oz) fresh shiitake mushrooms,
    stems discarded, caps thickly sliced

1 tablespoon vegetable oil
pinch of ground white pepper
pinch of sansho pepper
2 tablespoons Japanese soy sauce
2 tablespoons mirin
1 spring onion (scallion), extra, thinly
    sliced on the diagonal

Serves 4 as a main or 8 as a starter

To weight the tofu, wrap it in a clean tea towel. Put two plates on top of the tofu to extract any excess moisture and leave for about 1 hour. Remove from the tea towel, then pat dry with paper towels. Cut the block in half horizontally so you have two thin slices. Cut each of these slices into quarters so you have eight even cubes in total. Set aside.

Heat half the butter and sesame oil in a large, heavy-based frying pan over medium–high heat and add the garlic, ginger, spring onion and mushrooms to the pan and cook for 3–4 minutes, or until the mushrooms are softened. Remove from the pan.

Add the remaining butter and sesame oil with the vegetable oil to the pan. Season the tofu steaks well with salt, ground white pepper and sansho pepper and cook for about 6 minutes on each side, or until golden. Remove from the pan, cover and set aside.

Pour out the excess oil from the pan, leaving about 1 teaspoon. Increase the heat to high and add the soy sauce and mirin, then return the mushroom mixture to the pan. Mix well, then cook for 2 minutes, or until the mushrooms are heated through. Top each piece of tofu with the mushroom mixture and garnish with the extra spring onion. Serve immediately. Great with rice and green vegetables or a salad.

tofu steaks with mushrooms

japanese
chicken meatloaf

4 dried shiitake mushrooms
50 g (1¾ oz) lotus root
750 g (1 lb 10 oz) minced (ground) chicken
4 spring onions (scallions), chopped
3 garlic cloves, crushed
2 teaspoons finely grated fresh ginger
60 g (1 cup) panko (Japanese
   breadcrumbs)
1 egg
1 tablespoon Japanese soy sauce

1 tablespoon mirin
1 tablespoon white miso

GLAZE
2 tablespoons Japanese soy sauce
2 tablespoons mirin
1 teaspoon kuzu starch rocks or arrowroot

Serves 4 as a main or 8 as a snack

Soak the shiitake in hot water for 30 minutes, then drain. Discard the stems and finely chop the caps. If you are using fresh lotus, peel it, cut into 5 mm (¼ in) slices, then put in cold water.

Put the shiitake in a bowl with the chicken, spring onion, garlic, ginger, panko, egg, soy sauce, mirin and miso and mix well using your hands.

Lightly oil a 21 cm (8½ in) non-stick frying pan and add the mince mixture, patting down and smoothing over with damp hands. Arrange the lotus slices over the top, then press them down into the mince mixture.

Sit the pan over medium–low heat for about 20 minutes, or until it just starts to cook around the edges and the liquid is bubbling slightly. Increase the heat to high and cook for 4–5 minutes, or until the liquid has stopped bubbling and has almost evaporated. The meatloaf will have come away from the sides of the pan. Remove from the heat.

Meanwhile, to make the glaze, combine the soy sauce, mirin, kuzu and 2 tablespoons water in a small saucepan. Crush the kuzu with the back of a spoon and bring the mixture to the boil over medium–high heat, stirring until smooth, thick and glossy. Set aside.

Preheat the griller (broiler) to medium–high. Put the meatloaf under the heat and cook for 5 minutes. Brush with the glaze and cook for a further 6–8 minutes, brushing regularly with the glaze, or until the meatloaf is cooked through and is glossy on top. Remove from the heat and brush the remaining glaze over the top. Rest for 10 minutes, then cut into wedges and serve with salad.

KIRIN BI

¥1100	¥200	¥310	¥310	¥310	¥550	¥280	

— つめた〜い —

YEN
おれ入口

COIN
コイン投入口
500円硬貨も
使えます

おつり・返金 — お金はいつでももどります

¥

● 未成年者の飲酒は法律で
　禁じられています

● 飲酒運転はやめましょう

防犯装置付

午後11時〜午前5時

当店は酒類の
自動販売機の
時間制限を
厳守しております
店主

ER

¥220 ¥170 ¥170

上段の商品は A・B・C のボタンを押してくだ

KIRIN KIRIN SAPPORO KIRIN

¥280 ¥220 ¥220 ¥220

A B C

このボタンは上段の A・B・C の商品に対応します

トーザツルカップ。

未成年者の飲酒は法律
禁じられています

飲酒運転は
やめましょう

220円 170円

おつり・返却 投入口

当店
自動
時間
厳守

500 g (1 lb 2 oz) spaghetti or dried thin
    udon noodles
½ teaspoon sesame oil
1 teaspoon vegetable oil
3 streaky bacon rashers, thinly sliced
35 g (1¼ oz) butter
3 garlic cloves, thinly sliced
250 g (9 oz) fresh shiitake mushrooms,
    stems discarded, caps sliced
300 g (10½ oz) shimeji mushrooms,
    pulled apart

1½ tablespoons mirin
500 ml (2 cups) dashi II (page 245)
1½ tablespoons Japanese soy sauce
large pinch of ground white pepper
100 g (3½ oz) enoki mushrooms, ends
    trimmed and pulled apart
30 g (1 bunch) chives, thinly sliced

Serves 4

Bring a large saucepan of salted water to the boil. Add the spaghetti and cook according to the manufacturer's instructions until *al dente*. Drain, then rinse in cold water and drain well.

Heat the sesame and vegetable oils in a large, deep frying pan over medium–high heat, then add the bacon and cook for a few minutes, or until slightly crispy. Remove from the pan and set aside. Add most of the butter and all the garlic to the pan and cook for 1 minute, or until lightly golden. Immediately add the shiitake and shimeji mushrooms and stir for 2–3 minutes, or until just softened.

Add the mirin and cook for 1 minute, then add the dashi, soy sauce, white pepper and bacon to the pan, bring to the boil, then cook for 8 minutes, or until the liquid has reduced by half. Add the remaining butter, the enoki and the spaghetti to the pan and stir to combine and heat through. Season to taste with salt and freshly cracked black pepper. Divide among four deep noodle bowls and sprinkle with the chives. Serve immediately.

japanese spaghetti

omelettes
filled with rice

275 g (1¼ cups) Japanese short-grain rice
25 g (1 oz) butter
a few drops of sesame oil
1 onion, finely chopped
2 garlic cloves, crushed
2 teaspoons finely chopped fresh ginger
250 g (9 oz) chicken thigh fillets, diced
50 g (⅓ cup) frozen peas, thawed
125 ml (½ cup) tomato sauce (ketchup)

OMELETTES
8 eggs
2 teaspoons Japanese soy sauce
1 tablespoon mirin
1 teaspoon caster (superfine) sugar

CONDIMENTS *(optional)*
Japanese mayonnaise
tomato sauce (ketchup)

Serves 4 as a main

Rinse the rice several times in cold water until the water runs clear, then drain in a colander for 1 hour. Put in a saucepan with 375 ml (1½ cups) water. Bring to the boil, then cover with a tight-fitting lid, reduce the heat to low and simmer for 15 minutes. Turn off the heat but leave the pan on the hotplate. Working quickly, remove the lid, lay a clean tea towel over the top, then put the lid on and allow to sit for 15 minutes. Cool completely, then rinse well.

Melt the butter in a large frying pan, then add the sesame oil and onion and cook over medium heat for 8–10 minutes, or until golden. Add the garlic, ginger and chicken and cook, stirring, for 1 minute, or until the chicken starts to change colour. Add the peas and tomato sauce and mix well. Add the rice and mix again until the rice is evenly pink from the tomato sauce. Continue cooking, stirring occasionally, for about 5 minutes, until the chicken is cooked and the rice is completely heated through. Season to taste, then cover and set aside while you make the omelettes.

Lightly oil a Japanese omelette pan or non-stick frying pan and put over medium heat. Combine all the omelette ingredients in a bowl and lightly beat. Pour one-quarter of the egg mixture into the pan. Using chopsticks or a soft spatula, gently drag the outside edges of the egg into the centre until it just starts to set, then leave to cook for 1 minute. Spoon a quarter of the rice mixture along the centre line of the egg, then very carefully fold two sides towards the centre, over the rice, so you have a rectangular omelette. Put a serving plate over the top and very carefully invert the omelette onto the plate so the seam is on the bottom. Repeat with the remaining mixture to make four omelettes.

Serve with a little mayonnaise and tomato sauce, if you like.

60 ml (¼ cup) vegetable oil
1 bunch (about 6) baby leeks, cut into
　4 cm (1½ in) lengths
300 g (10½ oz) fresh shiitake mushrooms,
　stems discarded, caps cut in half if large
1 large onion, chopped
1 large carrot, peeled and chopped
4 streaky bacon rashers, chopped
2 tablespoons plain (all-purpose) flour
1 teaspoon ground sansho pepper
pinch of sea salt
1 kg (2 lb 4 oz) stewing beef, cut into
　large cubes
3 garlic cloves, crushed

375 ml (1½ cups) red wine
375 ml (1½ cups) sake
2 tablespoons red miso

MITSUBA MASH
1 kg (2 lb 4 oz) all-purpose potatoes,
　peeled and chopped
40 g (1½ oz) butter
200 ml (7 fl oz) cream
2 garlic cloves, crushed
10 g (½ cup) chopped mitsuba or flat-leaf
　(Italian) parsley

Serves 4–6 as a main

Heat 1 tablespoon of the oil in a large saucepan over medium heat, add the leeks and cook until lightly golden. Remove and set aside. Add the shiitake and cook for a few minutes, or until softened and browned slightly. Transfer to the leeks and set aside until ready to use. Add the onion, carrot and bacon to the saucepan and cook for 10 minutes, or until lightly browned. Remove and set aside, separate from the leeks.

Combine the flour, sansho pepper and sea salt in a bowl, then toss the beef in it to coat well.

Add a little more oil to the pan, then brown the beef in batches. Remove and set aside. Add the garlic to the pan and stir for a few seconds, then pour in the wine and sake and stir, scraping up any sediment stuck to the base of the pan. Return the beef to the pan with the bacon and vegetable mixture, the miso and 250 ml (1 cup) water. Increase the heat to high, stir until the miso dissolves, then bring to the boil. Reduce the heat to low, cover and simmer for 1½ hours, then add the leeks and shiitake and cook, uncovered, for a further 30 minutes, or until the beef is very tender and the sauce has thickened.

Meanwhile, to make the mash, cook the potatoes in salted boiling water for 20 minutes, or until tender, then drain. Combine the butter, cream and garlic in a small saucepan and heat gently until the butter melts. Mash the potatoes while you gradually pour in the cream mixture and continue mashing until smooth. Season to taste, then stir in the chopped mitsuba. Serve with the stew.

beef, shiitake and red wine stew

a little taste of...

Kissaten are Japanese-style coffee shops. The name is an abbreviation of *kitsu sa ten,* literally 'drink tea shop' but in reality it is a place where coffee and black tea are served along with light snacks. Black tea and coffee became known in Japan in the mid-nineteenth century, when the country was forced to open its doors after nearly three centuries of self-imposed isolation. Japan's first *kissaten* opened in Tokyo in 1888, and was a hit of the Western-influenced Meiji era. In the early twentieth century *kissaten* grew in fashion and number, and following the war years did so once again. During the late 1980s, the 'bubble era' of economic excess, a few became notorious for their excessive displays of luxury, offering costly coffee, perhaps sprinkled with flakes of gold, served in valuable European porcelain to ladies dressed in Chanel, seated on plush velvet and gazing upon a painting by Matisse. More recently, international coffee chains and European-style cafés have become established in Japan. These new pretenders are not to be confused with *kissaten,* which thrive on their more Japanese and genteel atmosphere, purveying their coffee and tea with delicate cakes and snacks.

...kissaten

green tea
ice cream

250 ml (1 cup) milk
625 ml (2½ cups) cream
1 vanilla bean, split in half lengthways
9 egg yolks
145 g (⅔ cup) caster (superfine) sugar
3 teaspoons matcha (green tea powder)

Makes 1 litre (4 cups)

Pour the milk and cream into a saucepan with the vanilla bean and bring just to the boil over medium–high heat. Remove from the heat and allow the vanilla to infuse into the milk mixture for 15 minutes.

Put the egg yolks and sugar in a bowl and beat until creamy. Slowly pour in the milk mixture, whisking as you pour, until smooth. Pour into a clean saucepan and put the pan over medium heat. Stir for 10 minutes, or until it is just thick enough to coat the back of a spoon.

Place the matcha in a small bowl, then stir in enough of the hot custard to form a paste, then add to the rest of the custard, whisking until smooth and an even green colour. Strain through a fine sieve and cool slightly. Cover and refrigerate until completely chilled, then churn in an ice cream machine according to the manufacturer's instructions. Place in the freezer until ready to use. If making by hand, freeze until frozen around the edges but not in the centre, then whisk with an electric whisk to break down any ice crystals. Return to the freezer and repeat this process at least twice more. The more times it is beaten while freezing the finer and silkier the finished ice cream texture will be. The finished ice cream should be light not icy.

4 small nashi, peeled, cored and sliced
1 tablespoon lemon juice
2 teaspoons finely grated fresh ginger
30 g (½ cup) panko (Japanese
    breadcrumbs)
230 g (1 cup) caster (superfine) sugar
40 g (¼ cup) white sesame seeds, lightly
    toasted, plus extra, to garnish
50 g (½ cup) walnuts, very finely chopped

1½ teaspoons ground cinnamon
1 teaspoon ground ginger
8 sheets filo pastry
150 g (5½ oz) butter, melted
2 tablespoons icing (confectioners') sugar
2 tablespoons kinako (roasted soya bean
    powder), for dusting

Serves 6–8

Preheat the oven to 180°C (350°F/Gas 4). Put the nashi slices in a bowl with the lemon juice, fresh ginger, panko and half the sugar and stir well. Combine the sesame seeds, walnuts, cinnamon, ground ginger and remaining sugar in a separate small bowl.

Lay one sheet of filo on a work surface with the long edge towards you, then brush lightly with a little melted butter, laying another sheet on top so it overlaps the edge furthest away from you by about 5 cm (2 in). Brush with a little more butter. Sprinkle about one-quarter of the sesame mixture over the top of the two pastry sheets, then keep layering in the same position with the rest of the filo and sesame mix, brushing each sheet of pastry with melted butter.

Leaving a 4 cm (1½ in) border on the edge of the pastry closest to you and on both sides, place the nashi mixture in a neat log along the edge closest to you. Carefully roll up, folding in the sides about halfway then continue rolling to the end.

Carefully transfer the strudel to a lightly greased baking tray, seam-side down and brush all over with a little melted butter. Bake for 50 minutes, or until golden. Allow to cool slightly before sprinkling with sifted combined icing sugar and kinako. Slice on the diagonal and serve with lightly whipped cream, if desired.

nashi and ginger strudel

pancakes with
sweet red bean paste

125 g (1 cup) plain (all-purpose) flour
1 teaspoon baking powder
2 tablespoons caster (superfine) sugar
2 eggs
125 ml (½ cup) milk
25 g (1 oz) butter
1 tablespoon oil
150 g (½ cup) anko (sweet adzuki bean
   paste)

Makes 6

Sift the flour and baking powder into a bowl and stir in the sugar. Combine the eggs and milk and whisk well. Make a well in the flour and add the egg mixture and stir until well combined.

Heat a little of the butter and oil in a frying pan over medium–high heat until the butter is melted. Cooking in batches, drop about 2 tablespoons of the batter per pancake (spread to a diameter of 9 cm/3½ in) into the pan and cook for 2 minutes, or until there are lots of bubbles on the surface. Turn over and cook a further 30 seconds. Don't worry if the first couple don't work. Remove from the pan, cover and set aside while you cook the remaining pancakes. You should end up with 12 good pancakes.

Sandwich two pancakes together with about 1 tablespoon of the red bean paste and repeat with the remaining pancakes and filling. Serve warm or at room temperature with green tea as an afternoon or after-dinner treat.

tea... So essential and beloved is green tea for the Japanese that it is rarely written or spoken of without the honorific *o* prefix. Fresh *o-cha* is prepared at home and in offices at least several times a day. Canned and bottled, it is sold in great quantities from every supermarket, convenience store, railway kiosk and beverage vending machine in the land.

Plantations of *Camellia sinensis* range over hillsides in the temperate tea-growing regions of Japan. The leaves, sometimes still picked by hand, are sterilized with steam to prevent fermentation, thereby retaining their natural flavour and characteristic green colour. Rolled and dried, they are ready to be briefly infused in hot water, and then drunk plain, always without milk or sweetening. Tea connoisseurs eagerly await each year's *shincha,* the 'new tea' from the first-growth leaves, which, when brewed, has a brighter colour and more mellow taste than older or second- or third-growth tea.

First introduced from China along with Buddhism in the sixth century, tea was initially valued for its medicinal properties and as an aid to meditation. Japanese monks studying in China later brought home the seeds from which today's bushes of *honcha,* 'true tea', are descended.

From the austere Zen temple tea rituals, *sado,* 'the way of tea', developed into a grand ceremonial style among the aristocracy. This transformation was opposed by proponents of a modest approach to the ritual which emphasizes the spiritual aspect of this communion. Both philosophies survive to this day in tea schools led by men who can trace their ancestral lineage back to the renowned sixteenth-century tea master Sen-no Rikyu.

Sado requires a fine tea powder called *matcha*, ground from the young leaves of aged tea bushes that have been specially tended. In this intricate symbolism-filled ceremony, the tea is not steeped but rather is vigorously whisked into a thick, frothy beverage using a beautiful *chasen* (whisk) of finely split bamboo. It is prepared and served in a bowl of apparent simplicity but often considerable artistic value.

145 g (⅔ cup) caster (superfine) sugar
a strip of lemon or lime zest
5 teaspoons gelatine granules
250 ml (1 cup) Midori or other green
  melon-flavoured liqueur

GREEN FRUIT SALAD
3 kiwi fruit
¼ small ripe honeydew melon, seeds
  removed
180 g (1 cup) green grapes

Serves 8

Place the sugar, zest and 625 ml (2½ cups) water in a saucepan and stir over high heat until it comes to the boil. Reduce to a simmer and cook for 10 minutes.

Place the gelatine in a small bowl and stir in some of the hot liquid until a smooth paste has formed. Pour back into the liquid in the pan and whisk until the gelatine has dissolved. Strain through a fine sieve and allow to cool.

Stir in the Midori until well combined, then divide among eight short drinking glasses or small glass bowls. Refrigerate for about 3 hours, or until set.

To make the fruit salad, peel the kiwi fruit and the melon and cut into 1.5 cm (⅝ in) dice. Place in a bowl, add the grapes and toss to combine. Spoon on top of the jelly and serve immediately with lightly whipped cream or green tea ice cream (page 231).

midori jelly with green fruit salad

plum wine granita

115 g (½ cup) caster (superfine) sugar
a few strips of lemon zest
2 cm (¾ in) piece of fresh young ginger,
   thinly sliced
500 g (1 lb 2 oz) ripe plums, seeded
500 ml (2 cups) Japanese plum wine
sliced fresh ripe plums, optional

Serves 6

Combine the sugar with the lemon zest, ginger and 375 ml (1½ cups) water. Stir over high heat until the sugar has dissolved, then bring to the boil. Reduce the heat to low and simmer for 10 minutes. Cool completely, then strain.

Purée the plum flesh in a food processor, then strain through a fine sieve to extract the juice (about 250 ml/1 cup). Add to the cooled syrup with the plum wine, then pour into a shallow 30 x 20 cm (12 x 8 in) metal container. Place in the freezer until the mixture begins to freeze around the edges.

Scrape the frozen sections back into the mixture with a fork. Repeat every 30 minutes, until the mixture has even sized ice crystals. Just before serving, beat the mixture with a fork, then spoon into six glasses. If you like, serve with slices of fresh plum.

basics

SUSHI RICE

550 g (2½ cups) Japanese
  short-grain white rice
4 cm (1½ in) piece of
  konbu, wiped with a damp
  cloth, optional
2 tablespoons sake, optional
80 ml (⅓ cup) Japanese
  rice vinegar

1½ tablespoons caster
  (superfine) sugar
½ teaspoon salt

Makes 6 cups

Rinse the rice several times in cold water or until the water runs clear, then drain in a colander for 1 hour.

Put the rice in a saucepan with 750 ml (3 cups) cold water and, if you wish, add the konbu and sake. Bring to the boil, then remove the konbu. Cover with a tight-fitting lid, reduce the heat to low and simmer for 15 minutes. Turn off the heat but leave the pan on the hotplate. Working quickly, remove the lid and place a clean tea towel across the top (to absorb excess moisture), then put the lid on for a further 15 minutes. Alternatively, cook the rice in a rice cooker, following the manufacturer's instructions.

Tip the rice into a wide, shallow non-metallic container and spread it out. Combine the vinegar, sugar and salt until the sugar is dissolved, then sprinkle over the warm rice. Using quick, short strokes mix the rice and liquid together with a damp wooden rice paddle or thin wooden spoon or spatula, being careful not to mush the rice. Traditionally the rice is cooled with a hand-held fan while mixing the liquid into the rice.

When cooled, cover with a clean, damp tea towel. For the best results, use the rice immediately and do not refrigerate it. However, if you are not making your sushi within 1–2 hours, the rice must be refrigerated or bacteria may develop.

DASHI I

10 cm (4 in) square piece of konbu
20 g (1 cup) katsuobushi (bonito flakes)

Makes about 1 litre (4 cups)

Wipe the konbu with a damp cloth but do not rub off the white powdery substance that will become obvious as it dries. Cut the konbu into strips.

Place the konbu and 1.5 litres (6 cups) cold water into a saucepan and slowly bring to the boil, then remove the konbu. Quickly add 60 ml (¼ cup) cold water to stop the boiling process. Add the bonito flakes, then allow it to return to the boil. Remove from the heat.

Allow the bonito flakes to sink to the bottom of the pan, then strain the liquid through a fine sieve. This stock is now ready for making clear soups.

DASHI II

10 cm (4 in) square piece of konbu
20 g (1 cup) katsuobushi (bonito flakes)

Makes about 1 litre (4 cups)

Wipe the konbu with a damp cloth but do not rub off the white powdery substance that will become obvious as it dries. Cut the konbu into strips.

Place the konbu and 1.5 litres (6 cups) cold water into a saucepan and slowly bring to the boil. Quickly add 60 ml (¼ cup) cold water to stop the boiling process. Add the bonito flakes, then allow it to return to the boil and simmer for 15 minutes. Remove from the heat.

Allow the bonito flakes to sink to the bottom of the pan then strain the liquid through a fine sieve. This stock is now ready for stews and thick soups.

INSTANT DASHI

**1–2 teaspoons instant
dashi granules**

Makes 1 litre (4 cups)

For instant dashi I, combine 1 teaspoon instant dashi granules with 1 litre (4 cups) boiling water and stir until dissolved. For instant dashi II, combine 2 teaspoons instant dashi granules with 1 litre (4 cups) boiling water and stir until dissolved.

KONBU DASHI

**15 cm (6 in) square
piece of konbu**

Makes 1.25 litres (5 cups)

For konbu dashi I, cut the konbu into strips and place in a saucepan with 1.5 litres (6 cups) cold water. Bring to the boil, then remove the konbu.

For konbu dashi II, leave the konbu in the pot, reduce to a simmer and cook for 10 minutes longer.

PONZU

**1 tablespoon lemon juice
1 tablespoon lime juice
1 tablespoon rice vinegar
60 ml (¼ cup) Japanese
    soy sauce
1 tablespoon mirin
60 ml (¼ cup) sake**

**1 teaspoon sugar
4 cm (1½ in) square piece of konbu,
    wiped with a damp cloth and cut
    into strips
1 tablespoon katsuobushi (bonito flakes)**

Makes about 250 ml (1 cup)

Place all ingredients in a non-metallic bowl and stir until the sugar is dissolved. Cover with plastic wrap and refrigerate for 24 hours. Strain through muslin or a fine sieve before using.

TEMPURA BATTER

310 ml (1¼ cups) iced water
45 g (¼ cup) potato starch, sifted
140 g (1 cup, plus 1 tablespoon) plain (all-purpose) flour, sifted
¼ teaspoon baking powder
¼ teaspoon salt

Makes 1 quantity

Pour the water into a bowl. Add the sifted potato starch, flour, baking powder and salt all at once and just give a few light strokes with a pair of chopsticks to loosely combine. There should be flour all around the edges of the bowl and the batter should be lumpy. (If your kitchen is hot, place over a bowl of iced water.)

TEMPURA DIPPING SAUCE

310 ml (1¼ cups) dashi II
60 ml (¼ cup) mirin
80 ml (⅓ cup) Japanese soy sauce

Makes 685 ml (2¾ cups)

Combine all the ingredients in a small saucepan and bring to the boil over high heat. Reduce the heat to low and keep warm until ready to serve.

GINGER JUICE

40 g (1½ oz) fresh ginger, peeled

Makes 1 tablespoon

Grate the ginger on a Japanese ginger grater, then squeeze the grated ginger with your fingertips to release the juice.

glossary

abura-age Deep-fried sheets of tofu that should be rinsed with boiling water to remove excess oil before use in simmered dishes, such as soups or stews. The sheets can also be sliced and used in stir-fries. *Inari abura-age* (see picture, page 151) are sheets of tofu that have been simmered in a sweet soy broth. These prepared sheets are used to make *inarizushi*.

anko Also called *an*. A sweet bean paste made by slow-cooking adzuki beans in a sugar syrup. It is used for filling Japanese confectionery and desserts.

bamboo shoots Also called *takenoko*. The young, pale shoots of certain bamboo, which have a mellow flavour. The fresh ones require some preparation before use, but the precooked, tinned ones are easier because they can be used as they are (see picture, page 157).

black sugar Also called *kurozato*. A dark brown sugar with a rich molasses flavour, usually sold in small rough lumps or rocks. It is commonly used to make a syrup, which is sometimes available pre-prepared, for use in traditional Japanese sweets. The lumps are sometimes added to simmered savoury dishes, particularly those with a Chinese influence. Crush the lumps before use.

chawan mushi cup The lidded ceramic cup used to cook the steamed Japanese custard of the same name. Difficult to find outside Japan, it may be substituted with a small Asian rice or soup bowl.

daikon A mildly flavoured giant white radish. It is an important staple of the Japanese diet. Raw daikon is finely grated for dipping sauces or dressings and shredded for salads. Daikon is believed to aid the digestion of oily foods. Daikon can have a pungent aroma, not dissimilar to cabbage, when cooked and it can become bitter with age. The leaves can be used in stir-fries or soups. Daikon has a high water content and is very porous. To store daikon, wrap it with plastic wrap and refrigerate to prevent from drying out. See picture, page 109.

dashi granules Made from konbu and *katsuobushi* and available also in powder form, this is an instant version of the essential Japanese stock, dashi.

edamame Young soya beans in the pod, available fresh when in season; otherwise frozen. See picture, page 32.

enoki mushroom A Japanese mushroom with a long, thin white stem and tiny white cap. Enoki mushrooms grow in clumps and can be pulled apart quite easily. They require very little cooking and can be eaten raw in salads. See picture, page 223.

ginkgo nut Also called *ginnan*. Not strictly a nut, this is the very small and pale yellow fruit of the *Ginkgo biloba* tree. Fresh ginkgo nuts have a crisp shell that must be removed. The pre-prepared tinned (see picture, page 58), frozen or vacuum-packed nuts are easier to use than the fresh. Cooked ginkgo nuts have a creamy, nutty flavour and slightly chewy texture.

gobo The long root of edible burdock. It is about 2–3 cm (¾–1¼ in) in diameter, found fresh in season with a very thin brown skin that needs to be lightly scraped or scrubbed off to reveal the cream coloured flesh. It is also available pre-scraped, cut and frozen ready for use. It has a wonderful earthy flavour, a little like a Jerusalem artichoke and is great in soups and simmered dishes. *Gobo* is high in dietary fibre and is believed to aid digestion. See picture, page 122.

harusame Also called spring rain noodles. These are very thin, clear noodles of Chinese origin, usually made from mung bean starch, but sometimes made from potato starch or sweet potato starch. They are popular in stews, hotpots and soups and are sometimes finely chopped as a coating for fried foods because they puff up and turn white when they hit the hot oil. See picture, page 36.

ichimi togarashi This is a chilli powder made from the dried *togarashi* chilli, a hot red Japanese pepper. It is used predominantly for sprinkling over soups, noodles and simmered dishes. See picture, page 20.

Japanese curry powder Also called *kare ko*. A flavoursome, aromatic curry powder available in varying degrees of heat. It can be substituted with Indian curry powder.

Japanese grater Also called *oroshigane*. There are two main types of graters used in Japanese cuisine. One is a flat grater with fine raised spikes perfect for grating ginger or wasabi into a paste (see picture, page 247). This type will often have a lip to catch the ginger juice, which is a common ingredient in Japanese cuisine. The second type of grater has slightly larger teeth and is used predominantly for grating daikon. Both styles are available in ceramic, plastic or stainless steel. Western-style graters are not an appropriate substitute as their teeth or holes are not fine enough.

Japanese mayonnaise It has a slightly salty–sweet egg flavour and contains soya bean oil. The most superior brand is called variously QP, kyuupii or kewpie

mayonnaise. It comes in a soft squeeze bottle with a star-shaped nozzle.

Japanese mustard Also called *karashi*. It looks and tastes a little like English mustard but is hotter and spicier. It should be used sparingly. Serve as a condiment or add to dressings.

Japanese rice vinegar Also called *komesu*. Made from vinegar and a natural rice extract, this slightly sweet and refreshing vinegar is less sharp than other types. Used in dressings and marinades. Choose a Japanese brand when cooking Japanese food.

Japanese short-grain rice A short-grained rice with a high starch content. When cooked, the rice is a little sticky, but still firm to the bite.

Japanese soy sauce Also called *shoyu*. A refined Japanese soy sauce. Available in heavy and light varieties, the heavier is less salty and slightly sweeter than light. Light soy sauce is more often used in cooking and the heavy is more often used as an accompaniment. They are suitable substitutes for each other.

kamaboko A small white loaf of steamed fish paste, made from the flesh of a variety of fish, processed with starch to help hold its shape. It comes attached to a small wooden board and is sometimes tinted bright pink. It should be sliced before eating and requires little cooking to warm through. Usually added at the end of cooking to simmered dishes. It can also be grilled (broiled). See picture, page 103.

kanpyo Also called *kampyo*. The pale flesh of a bottle-shaped gourd, cut into long thin strips, then dried. It must be fully rehydrated before use and, as it has little flavour of its own, should be cooked with other flavours, which it readily absorbs. Prepared *kanpyo* has been simmered in a sweet soy-based sauce ready for use in various sushi or as an appetizer with drinks or even as an edible tie for bundles of vegetables in vegetarian cuisine.

katakuriko A starch made from a plant called Japanese dog tooth violet. It is valued for the way it thickens sauces, resulting in a smooth, clear sauce. It also makes for a crispy coating on deep-fried foods. It can be quite expensive so is often substituted with potato starch.

katsuobushi The dried, smoked and cured flesh of the bonito, a member of the tuna family. It has a strong aroma but a smoky mellow flavour. It is usually shaved into large flakes (see picture, page 42) before using as a base for home-made dashi or shaved into smaller flakes (see picture, page 163) for garnishing.

kinako A flour made from ground, roasted soya beans with a slightly sweet nutty flavour. It is a common ingredient of traditional Japanese confectionery and desserts.

konbu Also called *kombu*. A dried kelp essential for making dashi. It can turn bitter if cooked for very long so it is often simply soaked overnight to add flavour to cooking liquid. Tasting of the sea and packed full of vitamins and minerals, dried *konbu* strips can be grilled, deep-fried or simmered in sweet soy sauce as a healthy snack food. *Konbu* comes covered with a white powdery substance. Wipe with a damp cloth to remove any grit, but do not wash. See picture, page 198.

konnyaku A gelatinous paste made from the starchy root of the konjac plant, it is formed either into blocks or 'noodles' called *shirataki*. It comes in white or speckled grey. It has little flavour or nutritional value but no fat and, as it readily absorbs surrounding flavours, it is often used as a bulking ingredient or for texture. Commonly used in simmered dishes and sometimes salads, it should always be boiled before eating. See picture, page 121.

kuzu A high-quality thickening starch made from the kudzu or kuzu vine. It is added to sauces to help them glaze well, used to set foods and even to make certain noodles. It comes as a powder or as small rocks, which should be crushed before use. It is often labelled, or substituted with, arrowroot. See picture, page 41.

lotus root Also called *renkon*. A rhizome with a crisp texture and a delicate, fresh flavour. It has small holes through the centre and, when sliced, looks like a flower. Once sliced, submerge it in vinegared water so it does not discolour. Fresh lotus root needs to be cooked before eating. It is also available peeled, thickly sliced and frozen, and in vacuum packs. See picture, page 184.

mandolin A chopping utensil that comes accompanied by various blade attachments or 'combs', which enable shredding or julienning.

matcha Fine green powder made from grinding high-grade green tea. It is the essential element of the Japanese tea ceremony. It must be whisked with hot water before drinking. It is also used to flavour Japanese confectionery, desserts and some soba noodles.

mirin Pale gold in colour, mirin is a sweet spirit-based rice liquid sometimes referred to as sweet rice wine. It is manufactured for use in cooking rather than drinking. It is commonly used in sauces, dressings and marinades. Look for bottles labelled *hon mirin* 'true mirin'. See picture, page 131.

miso A rich, earthy paste made from fermented soya beans. There are different grades and colours of miso. Generally the lighter the colour, the sweeter and less salty the taste. The base flavour in miso soup, it is also added to other dishes. The names are a little misleading as white miso (*shiromiso*) is pale gold, while red miso (*akamiso*) is a mid caramel colour with a reddish tinge. Brands can vary in colour and quality and be confusingly labelled. Since white and red miso can look quite similar, compare the colours when you are buying them. *Shinshu* is an all-purpose yellowish miso that makes a good substitute in most circumstances. *Hatcho miso* is dark reddish brown with a very strong, salty flavour. It should be used sparingly. Don't confuse it with red miso.

mitsuba Also known as trefoil or Japanese parsley. This is a long thin-stemmed herb with three leaves, resembling coriander (cilantro) or flat-leaf (Italian) parsley. It has a fresh, lightly peppery flavour similar to chervil and cucumber and is used predominantly in soups and salads. If not in season it can be substituted with flat-leaf parsley. See picture, page 67.

mizuna A large-leafed peppery herb with slight mustardy flavour, used in salads and sometimes added to simmered dishes. If not in season it can sometimes be substituted with rocket (arugula). See picture, page 204.

nashi A type of round Japanese pear with firm, sweet flesh. The slightly rough texture of the skin can vary in colour from pale yellow–green to brown. The darker the colour, the richer the flavour of the flesh. See picture, page 233.

nori Green paper-like sheets, the result of compressing and drying a particular marine algae found on the surface of the sea off Japan, China and Korea. It is a popular wrap for sushi and is often sold in pre-cut and toasted squares or rectangles specifically for this purpose. Also available in strips or flakes (*ao-nori*) for garnishing other savoury foods. See picture, page 26.

panko Crisp white breadcrumbs available in fine and coarse grades. Usually larger than traditional breadcrumbs, they make a very crisp coating for deep-fried foods. See picture, page 200.

pickled ginger Also called *gari*. Thinly sliced ginger that has turned pink in the pickling process. It has a sharp but sweet and refreshing flavour. It is used as a palate refresher with sashimi or sushi and can be chopped and added to cooked dishes for flavour or as a garnish. Some versions of pickled ginger are tinted a deeper reddish pink with food colouring but this is considered inferior and has a less refined flavour than the other. See picture, page 84.

plum wine Also called *umeshu*. This is a sweet liqueur with an almond flavour. It is made from *ume*, a Japanese apricot, which, curiously, is more often referred to as a plum. It is usually drunk neat or on the rocks but is also used as a flavouring for desserts. See picture, page 240.

ponzu The name of a dressing or dipping sauce combining lemon juice with soy sauce, *katsuobushi* and other flavourings. Ponzu is available commercially, but to make your own, see the recipe on page 246.

potato starch A thickening starch with similar qualities to *katakuriko*. Because potato starch is cheaper than *katakuriko* it is nowadays commonly used as a direct substitute. It is great for thickening sauces and coating deep-fried foods to give extra crunch.

ramen noodles Thin yellow noodles made from wheat flour and eggs. These noodles have a Chinese heritage. They are mainly used in soups. Available fresh, dried and instant.

sake An alcoholic liquid made by fermenting cooked, ground rice mash. It has a dry flavour, somewhere between vodka and dry sherry. In its less refined form it is light amber in colour and is used in cooking; however, there are many brands of good-quality, crystal clear sake available for drinking warm or cold.

sansho The ground seeds of the Japanese prickly ash, used as a pepper for sprinkling over or adding to foods. Its spicy aroma and flavour and slightly numbing quality demonstrate its close relation to Chinese Sichuan pepper. It is one of the seven spices that make up *shichimi togarashi*.

sesame oil This strongly flavoured oil extracted from roasted sesame seeds is used in dressings, for drizzling over foods and is also sometimes added to vegetable oil for flavour when stir-frying or deep-frying. A spicy version infused with chilli is popular for drizzling over noodle soups. Use sparingly.

sesame seeds Also known as *goma*. These are small, nutty-flavoured seeds. They are most often available in a cream colour but there is also a black variety, which is popular in Japan because of its value as a garnish. The oil-rich seeds are usually toasted to enhance the flavour before grinding to a paste for dressings or simply used as a garnish. See picture, page 131.

shichimi togarashi A spice mix containing seven different flavours. It always includes *togarashi*, a hot

red Japanese chilli. The remaining ingredients are flexible but often include mustard, sesame seeds, poppy seeds, sansho, shiso or nori flakes. It is mainly used for sprinkling over noodle soups, simmered dishes and grilled (broiled) foods as a garnish. See picture, page 158.

shiitake mushroom Perhaps the best known of the Japanese mushrooms, shiitake has a unique and relatively strong flavour. It has a flattish cap with edges that curl under. The woody stem should be discarded. Available fresh (see picture, page 116) or dried (see picture, page 137). The more pungent dried version is very similar to Chinese dried mushrooms. These must be rehydrated before cooking—the hard stem is usually discarded after the mushroom has been soaked.

shimeji mushroom A mushroom that grows in a cluster. The cluster can be easily pulled apart to reveal individual long-stemmed, pale-coloured mushrooms with small grey–brown caps. The mushrooms have a delicate flavour and are great in soups, simmered dishes, salads or stir-fries. See picture, page 100.

shirataki noodles Thin gelatinous 'strings' or noodles made from *konnyaku* that are added to soups, simmered and braised dishes. They can be substituted with *harusame* noodles.

shiso Also knows as perilla or beefsteak plant, shiso is a large-leafed herb with slightly ragged edges. It belongs to the mint family and has a flavour similar to basil. Available in dark green and, less commonly, in a purple–red colour, shiso is aromatic, refreshing and regularly used as an edible garnish for sushi and sashimi. Shredded shiso is great in soups or salads and the whole leaf is popular in tempura. The red version is used for flavouring and colouring umeboshi. See picture, page 48.

soba noodles Made from buckwheat flour, sometimes mixed with plain (all-purpose) flour, these thin, grey–brown noodles have a slightly nutty flavour and are often eaten on their own, cold with a dipping sauce or hot in a simple soy-flavoured broth. Available dried (see picture, page 10) and fresh, the fresh can be difficult to find outside Japan. They are sometimes flavoured with green tea, and are then known as *cha soba*.

somen noodles Fine white noodles made from wheat flour. They are usually eaten cold, often on a bed of rice, or in a light broth. Also popular in salads. See picture, page 29.

soya beans Available dried as small yellowish oval beans that require soaking before cooking, precooked in a can or fresh or frozen in the pod. They are rich in protein and are used in the manufacture of tofu, miso and soy sauce. See picture, page 32.

suribachi A Japanese mortar made from sturdy pottery. It has a ridged interior designed for efficient and easy grinding of ingredients, particularly sesame seeds. It comes with a wooden pestle or *surikogi*. See picture, page 106.

takuan Also called pickled daikon. Available whole or in pieces, usually tinted yellow with turmeric. It is great for serving alongside rich or oily dishes and rice as a delicious palate cleanser. See picture, page 77.

tamari A naturally fermented, thick, dark Japanese soy sauce with a stronger, sweeter flavour than Japanese soy sauce. Although true tamari is wheat free, there are many lesser brands that have misapplied the name. Check the label to be sure. Tamari is often sold in health food stores.

tofu Also called beancurd. Made by setting the 'milk' formed by soaking and grinding soya beans with water. Tofu is creamy and delicately flavoured and is available in a variety of textures, all with different uses. Silken tofu is very soft and fragile and is often used in sauces or desserts. Firm or cotton tofu (see picture, page 164) is a dense form of tofu that holds together well, which makes it ideal for stir-fries, stews, bakes or grills. Silken firm tofu (see picture, page 42) has a texture between the two and just holds together in slices or cubes for use in salads, soups or deep-frying but can just as easily be eaten with a spoon. Tofu is high in protein, so it is a popular inclusion in vegetarian cuisine.

udon noodles Thick white Japanese noodles made from wheat flour, available in various widths. The noodles are available both fresh and dried. Udon noodles are most often eaten in soups but they may also be served in braised dishes.

umeboshi A Japanese pickled plum, made from *ume*, actually a member of the apricot family. The small fruit is pickled in salt and vinegar and strongly flavoured and coloured a deep pinky red by the red shiso leaf. They are usually served as a simple, tart accompaniment to rice and other foods but can also be soaked and used in dressings. See picture, page 132.

wakame A curly leafed seaweed, usually dehydrated and broken into very small pieces. It swells considerably and quickly when added to water and has a soft texture, which can become slimy if left to soak for too long. It has a mild, pleasant green leafy vegetable taste. Use in soups and salads. See picture, page 19.

wasabi Wasabi paste is a hot, pungent mixture made from the knobby green root of the Japanese wasabi plant. It is also available in powdered form to be mixed to a paste when needed, and as a pre-prepared paste (see picture, page 87). It is sometimes referred to as Japanese horseradish because of its flavour but in fact it is not related to horseradish. The fresh root can be finely grated when in season and has a better flavour and less heat than wasabi paste. Use it sparingly as a condiment for sushi and sashimi and to add to dipping sauces to serve with noodles.

yakisoba noodles Chinese-style yellow egg noodles that are partly cooked and oiled ready for use. They are usually sold in plastic bags. If not available you can substitute with thin Hokkien noodles.

index

A

abura-age, 248
Agedashi dofu, see Agedashi tofu
Agedashi tofu, 42–3
anko, 248
Asparagus with egg yolk
    sauce, 124–5
Asupara kimizu, see Asparagus
    with egg yolk sauce

B

bamboo shoots, 248
Beans with sesame miso
    dressing, 130–1
beef
    Beef and potato stew, 176–7
    Beef and rice bowl, 166–7
    Beef, shiitake and red wine
        stew, 226–7
    Crumbed skewers, 56–7
    Glazed beef and vegetable
        rolls, 168–9
    Japanese hamburger, 214–15
    Rare beef with condiments, 48–9
    Sukiyaki, 164–5
    Yakisoba, 26–7
Bento box, 134–5
black sugar, 248
burdock, Sautéed, 122–3
burdock, see gobo
Buta jiru, see Pork and vegetable
    soup
Buta-no shogayaki, see Sautéed
    pork and cabbage

C

cabbage, Sautéed pork and,
    174–5
carrot salad, Daikon and, 108–9
Chawan mushi, see Savoury
    Japanese custard

chawan mushi cup, page 248
chicken
    Chicken and cracker
        salad, 210–11
    Chicken and egg rice
        bowl, 158–9
    Chicken and vegetable
        hotpot, 184–5
    Chicken hotpot, 196–7
    chicken meatloaf,
        Japanese, 218–19
    Chicken wing and soy bean
        stew, 180–1
    Deep-fried marinated
        chicken, 50–1
    Nabeyaki udon, 20–1
    Omelette filled with rice, 224–5
    Savoury Japanese
        custard, 58–9
    Simmered chicken
        meatballs, 190–1
    Teriyaki chicken, 172–3
    Yakitori, 40–1
Chikuzen-ni, see Chicken and
    vegetable hotpot
Chilled tofu with ginger and
    spring onion, 60–1
Chirashizushi, see Scattered sushi
Clear soup with scallops, 66–7
coleslaw, Japanese, 206–7
Corn with soy, 138–9
crab
    Crab, cucumber and wakame
        salad, 64–5
    Hand-rolled sushi, 82–3
Crumbed skewers, 56–7
cucumber and wakame
    salad, Crab, 64–5
cucumber salad, Somen noodle,
    prawn and, 28–9
curry, Japanese, 182–3

D

daikon, 248
Daikon and carrot salad, 108–9
daikon, Simmered, 128–9
dashi, 112–13, 245–6
dashi granules, 248
Deep-fried marinated chicken,
    50–1
Deep-fried prawns with dipping
    sauce, 70–1
desserts, 230–5, 238–41
Dorayaki, see Pancakes with
    sweet red bean paste
dumplings, Pork, 34–5

E

Ebi furai, see Deep-fried prawns
    with dipping sauce
edamame, 248, see also Fresh
    soya beans in the pod
egg rice bowl, Chicken and,
    158–9
egg yolk sauce, Asparagus with,
    124–5
eggplant with dashi, Grilled,
    112–13
enoki mushroom, 248

F

festival foods, 170–1
fish
    Crumbed skewers, 56–7
    Mixed hotpot, 102–3
    Salt-grilled fish, 68–9
    Tempura, 92–3
    Whole fish simmered in broth,
        98–9
    see also crab; prawns;
        salmon; scallops; tuna
fish market, 62–3
Five-flavoured rice, 154–5

Fresh soya beans in the pod, 32–3
Fried pork cutlet, 200–1
fried rice, Japanese, 156–7
fritters, Seafood and vegetable,
    94–5
fruit salad, Midori jelly with
    green, 238–9
Furofuki daikon, see Simmered
    daikon

G

Ginger juice, 247
ginkgo, 248
Glazed beef and vegetable
    rolls, 168–9
gobo, 248
Gomoku meshi, see Five-
    flavoured rice
granita, Plum wine, 240–1
grater, 248
Green tea ice cream, 230–1
Grilled eggplant with dashi,
    112–13
Gyoza, see Pork dumplings
Gyudon, see Beef and rice bowl
Gyuniku tataki, see Rare beef
    with condiments
Gyuniku yasai maki, see Glazed
    beef and vegetable rolls

H

hambaagaa, see Japanese
    hamburger
hamburger, Japanese, 214–15
Hand-moulded sushi, 74–5
Hand-rolled sushi, 82–3
Harumaki, see Japanese spring
    rolls
harusame, 248–9
Hiyayakko, see Chilled tofu with
    ginger and spring onion

hotpot
  Chicken, 196–7
  Chicken and vegetable,
    184–5
  Mixed, 102–3
  Salmon and miso, 100–1
Horenso no goma ae, see
    Spinach with sesame
    dressing, 106–7
Hotate no suimono, see Clear
    soup with scallops

I–J
ice cream, Green tea, 230–1
ichimi togarashi, 249
Inarizushi, see Sushi rice in
    pockets
Ishikari nabe, see Salmon
    and miso hotpot
izakaya, 30–49
Japanese chicken meatloaf,
    218–19
Japanese coleslaw, 206–7
Japanese curry, 182–3
Japanese curry powder, 249
Japanese fried rice, 156–7
Japanese grater, 249
Japanese hamburger, 214–15
Japanese mayonnaise, 251
Japanese mustard, 249
Japanese potato salad, 208–9
Japanese rice vinegar, 249
Japanese short-grain rice, 249
Japanese soy sauce, 249
Japanese spaghetti, 222–3
Japanese spring rolls, 36–7

K
Kabocha–ni, see Sweet
    simmered pumpkin
Kake soba, see Soba noodles in
    broth
Kake udon, see Udon noodles in
    broth
Kakiage, see Seafood and
    vegetable fritters
Kaku–ni, see 188–9
kamaboko, 249
Kani–su, see Crab, cucumber

and wakame salad
kanpyo, 249
Kare, see Japanese curry
katakuriko, 249
katsuobushi, 249
Kimpira gobo, see Sautéed
    burdock
kinako, 249
kinoko supagettei, see
    Japanese spaghetti
kissaten, 228–43
konbu, 249–250
Konbu dashi, 246
konnyaku, 250
Kushiage, see Crumbed skewers
kuzu, 250

L–M
lotus root, 250
Makizushi, see 76–7
mandolin, 250
matcha, 250
matcha aisukuriimu, see Green
    tea ice cream
meatballs, Simmered chicken,
    190–1
meatloaf, Japanese chicken,
    218–19
Midori jelly with green fruit
    salad, 238–9
mirin, 250
miso, 250
miso hotpot, Salmon and, 100–1
Miso ramen, 18–19
miso sauce, Poached pork
    with, 194–5
Miso shiru, see Miso soup
Miso soup, 144–5
mitsuba, 250
Mixed hotpot, 102–3
mizuna, 250
mushrooms, Tofu steaks
    with, 216–17
Mushrooms with ponzu
    dressing, 116–17
mustard, 250

N–O
Nabeyaki udon, 20–1

Namasu, see Daikon and carrot
    salad
nashi, 250
Nashi and ginger strudel, 232–3
Nikujaga, see Beef and potato
    stew
Nizakana, see Whole fish
    simmered in broth
noodle bar, 10–29
noodles, 16–17
nori, 250
O-bento, 134–5
Okinawan slow-cooked
    pork, 188–9
Okonomiyaki, see Savoury
    pancake
Omelette filled with rice, 224–5
omuraisu, see Omelette filled
    with rice
O–nigirizushi, see Hand-moulded
    sushi
Oshizushi, see Pressed sushi
Oyako donburi, see Chicken and
    egg rice bowl

P
pancake, Savoury, 198–9
Pancakes with sweet red bean
    paste, 234–5
panko, 250
pickled ginger, 251
pickles, 126–7
plum dressing, Pumpkin with
    pickled, 132–3
plum wine, 251
Plum wine granita, 240–1
Poached pork with miso
    sauce, 194–5
Ponzu, 246, 251
ponzu dressing, Mushrooms
    with, 116–17
pork
  Crumbed skewers, 56–7
  Fried pork cutlet, 200–1
  Japanese curry, 182–3
  Japanese hamburger, 214–15
  Japanese spring rolls, 36–7
  Okinawan slow-cooked
    pork, 188–9

Poached pork with miso
    sauce, 194–5
Pork and vegetable
    soup, 146–7
Pork dumplings, 34–5
Sautéed pork and
    cabbage, 174–5
Yakisoba, 26–7
potato salad, Japanese, 208–9
potato starch, 251
potato stew, Beef and, 176–7
prawns
  Deep-fried prawns with
    dipping sauce, 70–1
  Hand-moulded sushi, 74–5
  Mixed hotpot, 102–3
  Nabeyaki udon, 20–1
  Pressed sushi, 78–9
  Savoury Japanese custard,
    58–9
  Scattered sushi, 84–5
  Seafood and vegetable fritters,
    94–5
  Somen noodle, prawn and
    cucumber salad, 28–9
  Tempura, 92–3
Pressed sushi, 78–9
pumpkin, Sweet simmered,
    114–15
Pumpkin with pickled plum
    dressing, 132–3

R
ramen noodles, 18–19, 251
Ramen noodles with soy broth,
    14–15
Rare beef with condiments, 48–9
red bean paste, Pancakes with
    sweet, 234–5
rice, 152–3
  Beef and rice bowl, 166–7
  Chicken and egg rice
    bowl, 158–9
  Five-flavoured rice, 154–5
  Glazed beef and vegetable
    rolls, 168–9
  Japanese fried rice, 156–7
  Omelette filled with rice,
    224–5

Rice soup, 148–9
Sushi, 244
Sushi rice in pockets, 150–1
Rolled sushi, 76–7

S
sake, 46–7, 251
Sake batayaki, see Sake-glazed
    salmon
Sake-glazed salmon, 90–1
salad
    Chicken and cracker, 210–11
    Crab, cucumber and
        wakame, 64–5
    Daikon and carrot, 108–9
    Japanese coleslaw, 206–7
    Japanese potato, 208–9
    Somen noodle, prawn and
        cucumber, 28–9
    Tomato and tofu, 204–5
    White, 120–1
salmon
    Hand-rolled sushi, 82–3
    Sake-glazed salmon, 90–1
    Salmon and miso hotpot,
        100–1
    Salmon and tofu balls, 44–5
    Sashimi, 86–7
    Scattered sushi, 84–5
Salt-grilled fish, 68–9
sansho, 251
Sashimi, 86–7
Sautéed burdock, 122–3
Sautéed pork and cabbage,
    174–5
Savoury Japanese custard, 58–9
Savoury pancake, 198–9
Sayaingen no miso ae, see
    Beans with sesame dressing
scallops
    Clear soup with scallops,
        66–7
    Crumbed skewers, 56–7
    Mixed hotpot, 102–3
    Seafood and vegetable
        fritters, 94–5
Scattered sushi, 84–5
Seafood and vegetable fritters,
    94–5

seaweed, 88–9
sesame dressing, Spinach
    with, 106–7
sesame miso dressing, Beans
    with, 130–1
sesame oil, 251
sesame seeds, 251
shichimi togarashi, 251
shiitake and red wine stew,
    Beef, 226–7
shiitake mushroom, 251
Shiitake no nimono, see Shiitake
    simmered in soy
Shiitake simmered in soy, 136–7
shimeji mushroom, 251
Shio yaki zakana, see Salt-grilled
    fish
Shira ae, see White salad
shirataki noodles, 251
shiso, 251–2
Shoyu ramen, see Ramen
    noodles with soy broth
Simmered chicken meatballs,
    190–1
Simmered daikon, 128–9
Simmered tofu, 162–3
soba noodles, 252
Soba noodles in broth, 12–13
Soba noodles with dipping
    sauce, 10–11
Somen noodle, prawn and
    cucumber salad, 28–9
somen noodles, 252
soup
    Clear with scallops, 66–7
    Miso, 144–5
    Pork and vegetable, 146–7
    Rice, 148–9
soy, 192–3
    Corn with, 138–9
    Shiitake simmered in, 136–7
soya bean stew, Chicken wing
    and, 180–1
soya beans, 252
soya beans in the pod,
    Fresh, 32–3
soy broth, Ramen noodles
    with, 14–15
spaghetti, Japanese, 222–3

Spinach with sesame dressing,
    106–7
spring rolls, Japanese, 36–7
stew
    Beef and potato, 176–7
    Beef, shiitake and red
        wine, 226–7
    Chicken wing and soy
        bean, 180–1
stir-fry, Vegetable, 140–1
strudel, Nashi and ginger, 232–3
Sukiyaki, 164–5
suribachi, 252
sushi
    Hand-moulded, 74–5
    Hand-rolled, 82–3
    Pressed, 78–9
    Rolled, 76–7
    Scattered, 84–5
sushi bar, 72–3
Sushi rice, 244
Sushi rice in pockets, 150–1
Sweet simmered pumpkin,
    114–15

T
takuan, 252
tamari, 252
tea, 236–7
Temakizushi, see Hand-rolled
    sushi
Tempura, 92–3
Tempura batter, 247
Tempura dipping sauce, 247
Tenpura, see Tempura
Tentsuyu, 247
Teriyaki chicken, 172–3
tofu, 252
    Agedashi tofu, 42–3
    Chilled tofu with ginger and
        spring onion, 60–1
    Miso ramen, 18–19
    Salmon and tofu balls, 44–5
    Simmered tofu, 162–3
    Tofu dengaku, 52–3
    Tofu steaks with mushrooms,
        216–17
    Tomato and tofu salad, 204–5
    White salad, 120–1

Tomato and tofu salad, 204–5
Tomorokoshi batayaki, see Corn
    with soy
Tonkatsu, see Fried pork cutlet
Tonkatsu sauce, 200–1
Tori-no mizutaki, see Chicken
    hotpot
Tori–no tsukune–ni, see Simmered
    chicken meatballs
Tori tatsuta–age, see Deep-fried
    marinated chicken
Tori teriyaki, see Teriyaki chicken
tuna
    Sashimi, 86–7
    Scattered sushi, 84–5

U–V
udon noodles, 252
Udon noodles in broth, 22–3
umeboshi, 252
vegetable market, 104–5
Vegetable stir-fry, 140–1
Vegetarian dashi, 246
vegetarian food, 110–11

W–Z
wakame, 252
wakame salad, Crab, cucumber
    and, 64–5
wasabi, 252
Wasabi mayonnaise dipping
    sauce, 44
White salad, 120–1
Whole fish simmered in broth,
    98–9
Yakimeshi, see Japanese fried rice
Yakinasu, see Grilled eggplant
    with dashi
Yakisoba, 26–7
yakisoba noodles, 252
Yakitori, 40–1
yakitori bar, 38–9
yoshoku, 202–7
Yasai itame, see Vegetable stir-fry
Yosenabe, see Mixed hotpot
Yu–dofu, see Simmered tofu
Zaru soba, see Soba noodles
    with dipping sauce
Zosui, see Rice soup

First published in 2004 by Murdoch Books Pty Limited.
This edition published 2009.

Murdoch Books Australia
Pier 8/9, 23 Hickson Road, Millers Point, NSW 2000
Phone: + 61 (0) 2 8220 2000
Fax: + 61 (0) 2 8220 2558
www.murdochbooks.com.au

Murdoch Books UK Limited
Erico House, 6th Floor, 93/99 Upper Richmond Road
Putney, London SW15 2TG
Phone: + 44 (0) 20 8785 5995
Fax: + 44 (0) 20 8785 5985
www.murdochbooks.co.uk

Chief Executive: Juliet Rogers
Publishing Director: Kay Scarlett

Publisher: Lynn Lewis
Designer: Susanne Geppert
Cover Designer: Jacqueline Richards
Photographers: Gorazd Vilhar (location); Alan Benson (recipes)
Production: Kita George

National Library of Australia Cataloguing-in-Publication Data
Title: A little taste of Japan.
ISBN 978 1 74196 756 2 (pbk)
Notes: Includes index.
Subjects: Cookery, Japanese.
Dewey Number: 641.5952

IMPORTANT: Those who might be at risk from the effects of salmonella food poisoning (the elderly, pregnant women, young children
and those suffering from immune deficiency diseases) should consult their doctor with any concerns about eating raw eggs.

CONVERSION GUIDE: You may find cooking times vary depending on the oven you are using. For fan-forced ovens, as a general rule, set the
oven temperature to 20°C (35°F) lower than indicated in the recipe. We have used 20 ml (4 teaspoon) tablespoon measures. If you are using
a 15 ml (3 teaspoon) tablespoon, for most recipes the difference will not be noticeable. However, for recipes using baking powder, gelatine,
bicarbonate of soda (baking soda), small amounts of flour and cornflour (cornstarch), add an extra teaspoon for each tablespoon specified.